READING THE BIBLE
STUDY GUIDE

Book Summaries and Questions for Deeper Study

DR. BILL CREASY

ZONDERVAN
REFLECTIVE

ZONDERVAN REFLECTIVE

Reading the Bible Study Guide
Copyright © 2025 by William C. Creasy

Published in Grand Rapids, Michigan, by Zondervan. Zondervan is a registered trademark of The Zondervan Corporation, L.L.C., a wholly owned subsidary of HarperCollins Christian Publishing, Inc.

Requests for information should be addressed to customercare@harpercollins.com.

Zondervan titles may be purchased in bulk for educational, business, fundraising, or sales promotional use. For information, please email SpecialMarkets@Zondervan.com.

ISBN 978-0-310-17675-6 (softcover)
ISBN 978-0-310-17676-3 (ebook)

Published in association with Shannon Marven of the literary agency Dupree/Miller & Associates, Inc.

Cover design: Studio Gearbox
Cover images and part page images: Everett Collection / Shutterstock (pg. 1), © Tom-B (pg. 15), Ana Maria Creasy/Logos
    Education Corp. (pg. 75)
Interior design: Kait Lamphere

Contents

—— Part 1: Introduction ——

—— Part 2: The Old Testament ——

—— Part 3: The New Testament ——

Preface

I've been teaching the Bible for over thirty years, first on the UCLA English Department faculty, where my flagship course was the English Bible as Literature, and later in the broader community through my website, logosbiblestudy.com; my popular mobile app, Bible Beat; and on Audible.com, where my teachings have garnered thousands of five-star reviews. In every format, I've taught verse by verse through the entire Bible, Genesis through Revelation. As I contend in my book *Reading the Bible: A Literary Guide to Scripture*, the Bible is a unified literary work with a beginning, a middle, and an end. Its main character is God, its conflict is sin, and its theme is redemption. Read straight through, the Bible is the greatest story ever told, and it is a major work of world-class literature.

Many people have tried to read the Bible from cover to cover but have become bogged down, perhaps somewhere around Leviticus or Chronicles. The Bible is, after all, a big book rooted in ancient cultures very different from our own and written in ancient languages that most people don't know. To make the journey successfully, it's helpful to have a scout who knows the trail—one who has been down it many times and knows his way around the rocks, ruts, and thickets, one who can guide you fruitfully to the final chapter and verse. That has been my goal for the past thirty years: to guide my students to a deeper understanding of God's Word.

Image: Monkey Business/stock.adobe.com

Reading the Bible: A Literary Guide to Scripture is your map for the journey, and this workbook is your compass. You and I can make the journey together, walking at a comfortable pace, perhaps accompanied by your Bible study companions. It's a great adventure, so open your Bible and let's hit the trail!

Dr. C.

> When I found your words I devoured them;
>
> they became my joy and the happiness of my heart. (Jer. 15:16, my translation)

Opening Prayer

Dr. Creasy begins all of his Scripture classes with this opening prayer.
You may want to do so too!

Gracious Father,
We thank you for bringing us here today
To read and study your Word.
Please open our minds and hearts to what you have to say,
That in better understanding you,
We may come to love you more deeply.

God our Father,
You sent your Son into the world to be its true light.
Pour out the Holy Spirit he promised us,
To sow truth in our hearts
And awaken in us obedience to the faith.
May we all be born again to new life
And enter the fellowship of your holy people.

Grant this through our Lord, Jesus Christ, your Son,
Who lives and reigns with you and the Holy Spirit,
One God forever and ever.
Amen.

Introduction

In the preface to *Reading the Bible: A Literary Guide to Scripture*, I invited you to join me on a great adventure, reading verse by verse through the entire Bible, Genesis through Revelation. But before we start, let's get to know each other. I told you about me in the preface to this workbook, so now tell me and our fellow students about you.

1. On a scale of 1 to 10, rate your current knowledge of the Bible.

   Very little   1   2   3   4   5   6   7   8   9   10   Expert

2. What do you hope to gain from your Bible study? Check all the boxes that apply.
   - ☐ I want to develop a more intimate relationship with God and Jesus by getting to know them through a deeper understanding of Scripture.
   - ☐ I want to know the biblical characters as real living and breathing people.
   - ☐ I want to understand the Old and New Testaments in their proper historical and cultural context.
   - ☐ I want to understand what parts of the Bible are historically accurate.

Image: Dr. Creasy teaching on the Arbel Cliff overlooking the Sea of Galilee. *Ana Maria Creasy/ Logos Education Corp.*

- ☐ I want to distinguish the various genres of literature that comprise the Bible.
- ☐ I want to know how the books of the Bible got there in the first place.
- ☐ I want to be biblically literate.
- ☐ I want to impress my friends and family with my biblical knowledge.
- ☐ I want to know how reading Scripture can deepen my prayer life.
- ☐ I want to know how reading Scripture can improve my personal relationships.

3. On a scale of 1 to 10, rate what influenced you in developing the biblical knowledge you currently have.

My family
Very little 1   2   3   4   5   6   7   8   9   10   Very much

My church
Very little 1   2   3   4   5   6   7   8   9   10   Very much

My pastor
Very little 1   2   3   4   5   6   7   8   9   10   Very much

My friends
Very little 1   2   3   4   5   6   7   8   9   10   Very much

A former teacher
Very little 1   2   3   4   5   6   7   8   9   10   Very much

My own reading
Very little 1   2   3   4   5   6   7   8   9   10   Very much

4. What other factors influenced you in your Bible study?

5. If you were to give yourself a letter grade on your current biblical knowledge, what would that grade be?

— Discussion Questions —

1. How have you approached the Bible in your past Scripture study? Did you study the Bible on your own, or were you involved in a group Bible study? If you studied on your own, was it systematic or random? If you studied in a group, what Bible study program did you use? What were the strengths and weaknesses of your past Bible study?

2. What is your favorite book of the Bible? Why?

3. What is your least favorite book of the Bible? Why?

4. Who is your favorite character in the Old Testament? Why?

5. Who is your favorite character in the New Testament? Why?

— Part 1 —

INTRODUCTION

Chapter 1

Four Foundational Principles

1. The four foundational principles for understanding the Bible are:
   1. The Bible is rooted in _____.
   2. The Bible emerges from _____.
   3. The Bible is a _____.
   4. The Bible is the _____.

2. Write on the following map where these bodies of water are located:
   - ☐ Red Sea
   - ☐ Persian Gulf
   - ☐ Mediterranean Sea
   - ☐ Black Sea

Image: Dr. Creasy and his intrepid students hiking the forty-three-mile "Jesus Trail" from Nazareth to Capernaum. _Ana Maria Creasy/Logos Education Corp._

3. Write on the following map where these Old Testament people were located:

- ☐ Egyptians
- ☐ Babylonians
- ☐ Hittites
- ☐ Syrians

- ☐ Israel
- ☐ Ammonites, Moabites, Edomites
- ☐ Assyrians

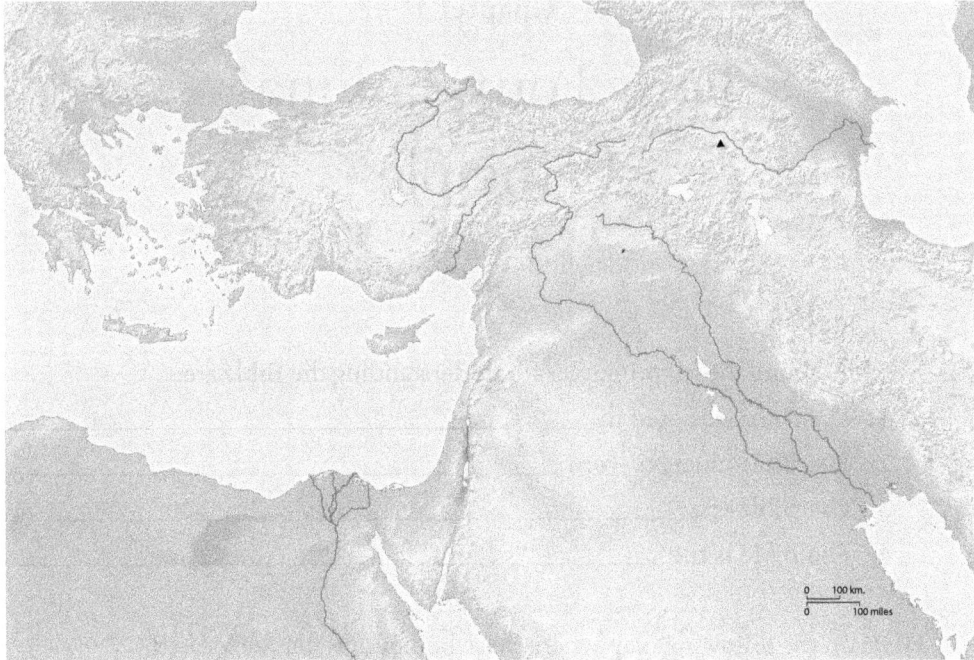

4. Write on the following map where these New Testament locations are found:

- ☐ Asia Minor
- ☐ Gaul
- ☐ Africa
- ☐ Egypt
- ☐ Macedonia

- ☐ Spain
- ☐ Greece
- ☐ Rome
- ☐ Jerusalem

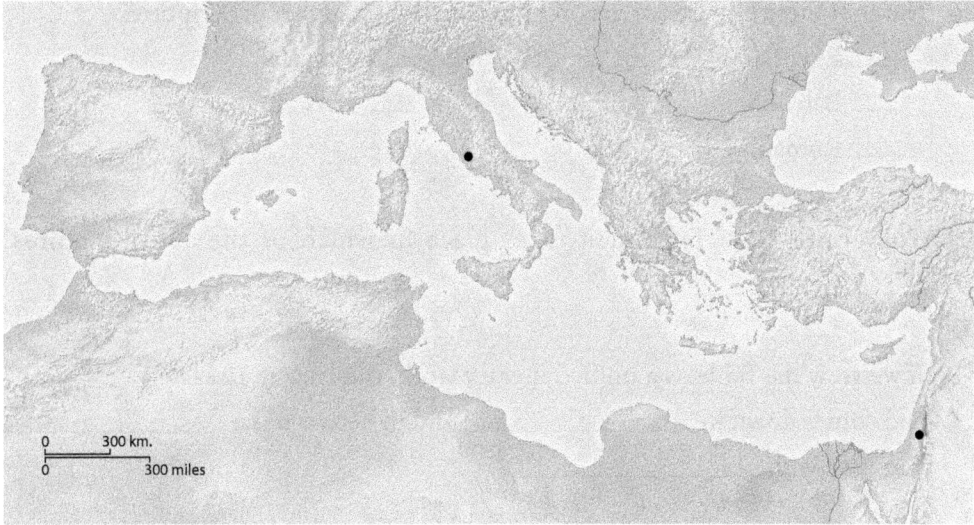

5. Identify the two inland bodies of water and the river connecting them on the map below.

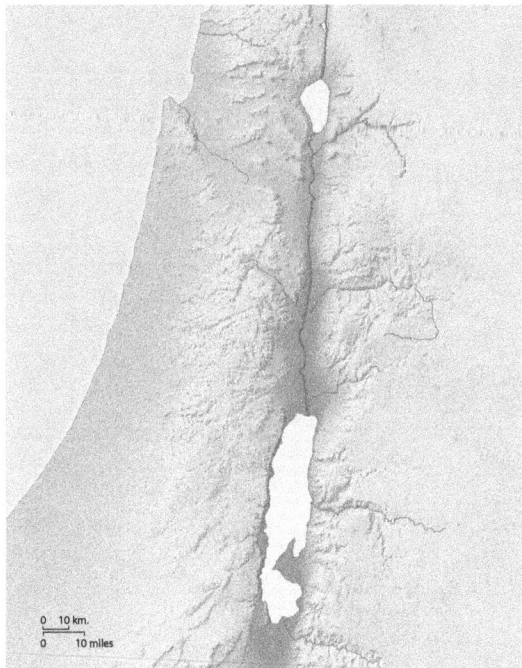

6. Number these empires in the order in which they appear in Scripture:

    ____ Egyptian   ____ Assyrian

    ____ Babylonian   ____ Persian

    ____ Roman

7. The entire New Testament takes place in which of the above empires?

    _____

8. If we view the Bible as a unified literary work, the curtain rises in _____ and comes down in _____, and in between is a _____ narrative with _____.

— Discussion Question —

The Bible is the Word of God. How do you understand that statement?

— Chapter 2 —

Writing the Bible

1. This chapter discusses two hypotheses regarding the Synoptic Gospels (Matthew, Mark, and Luke), the _____ approach and the _____ approach.

2. The traditional approach takes at face value that Matthew, Mark, and Luke wrote their own gospels, _____ being an eyewitness to the events of Jesus' life; _____ learning of Jesus' life from _____; and Luke having _____ everything carefully.

3. Although the _____ approach dominated much thinking in the late nineteenth century and throughout most of the twentieth century, other approaches have emerged, such as: _____, _____, _____, _____, _____, and _____, among others.

---

4. The form-critical approach assumes that the time and culture of Jesus' day were primitive—an _____ culture, not a literary culture.

5. It also assumes that a literary work such as a gospel _____ over time, the work of editors and redactors.

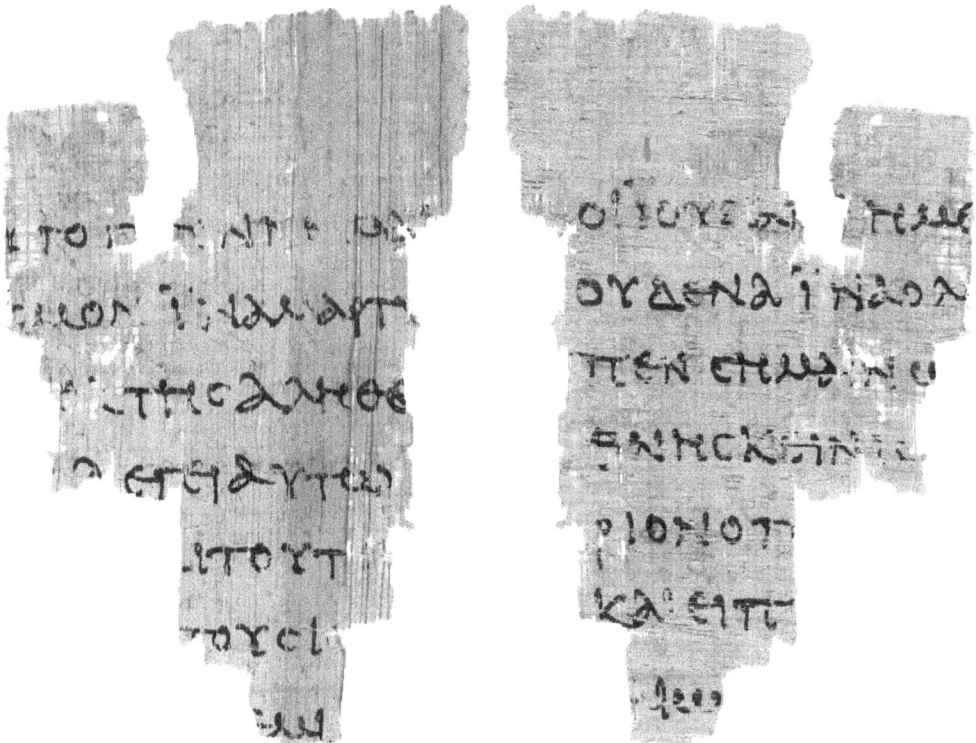

The oldest existing New Testament manuscript dates from AD 125. Only a papyrus fragment, it contains John 18:31–34 on one side (recto) and John 18:37–38 on the other side (verso). *Image provided by The John Rylands Research Institute and Library, The University of Manchester.*

— Discussion Questions —

1. If you were among Jesus' disciples and had witnessed his entire public ministry, how would you go about writing *your* gospel? Would you arrange it chronologically, like Matthew? Would you tell your story urgently, like Mark? Would you carefully research everything about Jesus like Luke? Or would you do something entirely different?

2. What do you regard as the key moments in Jesus' life, moments that define who he is? Would they be major events, or would they be small, insightful moments?

3. Of all the people mentioned in the Gospels, who would you most like to interview? Why?

4. Jesus had many women followers. If one of those women—say, Mary Magdalene—were to have written a gospel, how might it differ from the four gospels we have?

— Chapter 3 —

The Canon of Scripture

1. The word *canon* means a _____ or _____.

2. Writing in the West first developed around 3100 BC in both _____ and _____.

3. Those in the ancient world who knew how to write were called _____.

4. As writing developed and became more sophisticated, sacred texts evolved into _____ texts, works that explore the great questions of life.

5. Canons, whether musical, literary, or other, are not declared from on high; rather, they emerge over time by _____.

6. Old Testament books that did not make it into the biblical canon are called _____.

Image: Z. Radovan/BibleLandPictures.com

7. The third-century BC pseudepigraphical *Letter of Aristeas* tells the story of what?

8. What is the importance of the Dead Sea Scrolls?

9. For the first 350 years of Christianity, there was no agreed-upon canon of the New Testament. True or false?

   □ True   □ False

10. When did the church finally have an agreed upon canon of the books in the New Testament?

11. After the Council of Hippo in AD 393, what was the official Bible of Christendom for the next one thousand years?

12. What are books called that didn't make it into the New Testament canon?

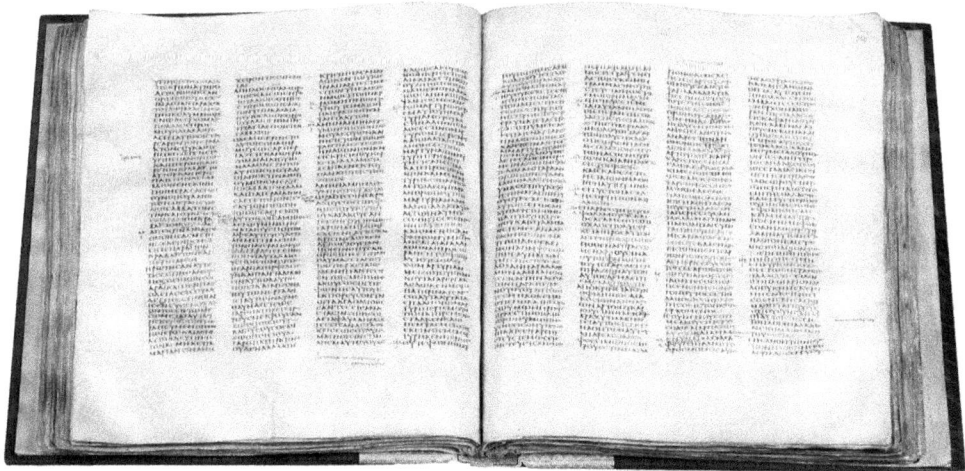

Codex Sinaiticus (Add MS 43725), uncial script on parchment, fourth century (after AD 325). This is the oldest complete copy of the Bible. British Library, London. *Z. Radovan/ BibleLandPictures.com*

— Discussion Question —

Orthodox Bibles have 52 books in the Old Testament and 27 books in the New Testament, for a total of 79 books.

Roman Catholic Bibles have 46 books in the Old Testament and 27 books in the New Testament, for a total of 73.

Protestant Bibles have 39 books in the Old Testament and 27 books in the New Testament, for a total of 66 books.

Why do you think that is?

Part 2

THE OLD
TESTAMENT

Chapter 4

Reading Genesis

Genesis is the story of beginnings: the beginning of creation, the beginning of human history, the beginning of sin, and the beginning of a family that plays a founding role in the story of redemption—that of Abraham and his descendants. After the primeval chapters 1–11, Genesis opens up like a tryptic with the Abraham and Isaac story (12:1–25:18), the Isaac and Jacob story (26:19–36:43), and the Jacob and Joseph story (37:1–50:26). Genesis is quite simply one of the greatest stories in ancient literature.

1. The first eleven chapters of Genesis, the creation story through the Tower of Babel, are classified as _____ literature.

2. Genesis 12–50 has an overall three-part structure: the _____ story; the _____ story; and the _____ story.

3. The Genesis story begins with _____, and it ends _____.

Image: Public domain/Library of Congress

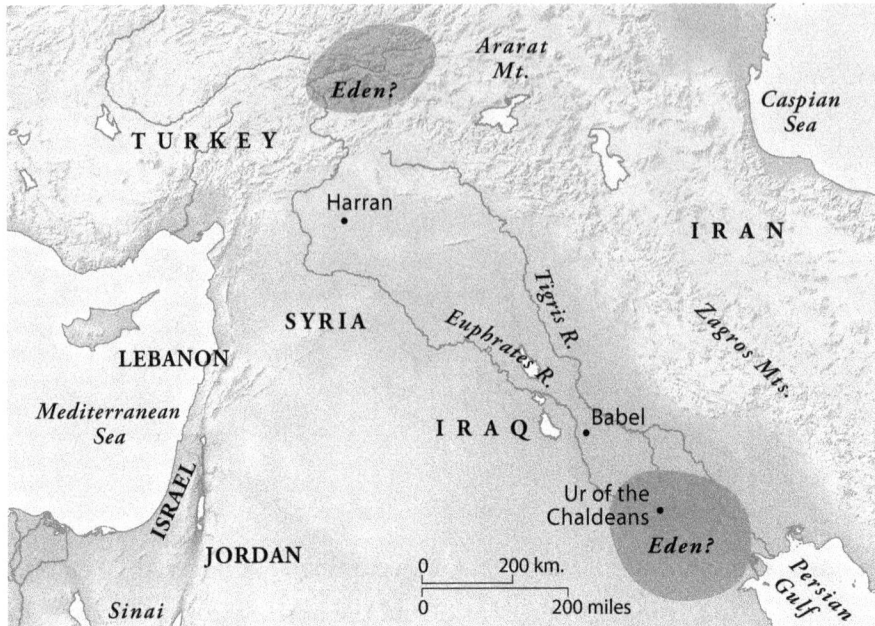

Setting of Genesis

4. The whole story of Joseph and his brothers hinges on _____.

5. When Joseph goes missing, what do his brothers say to their father, Jacob?

6. When the brothers meet Joseph in Egypt, why do they not recognize him?

7. The most unlikely hero in the Jacob and Joseph story is _____.

8. How does the story of Joseph tie in with the opening of the New Testament in Matthew's gospel?

The Ancient of Days, in *Europe: A Prophecy* by William Blake, 1794. *Public domain/Library of Congress*

— Discussion Questions —

1. The Bible consists of a variety of literary genres, each one with its own conventions. Genesis 1–11 is classified as mythopoeic literature. What are some of the conventions of this genre?

2. The superb biblical scholar Robert Alter, professor of Hebrew and comparative literature at the University of California, Berkeley, translated the entire Old Testament (*The Hebrew Bible: A Translation with Commentary* [New York: Norton, 2018]). In his book, he points out a grammatical crux in Genesis 1:1 that lies with the word רֵאשִׁית (*ray-sheeth'*, "beginning"), which is bound to an unmarked relative clause: there is no definite article *the*, so grammatically רֵאשִׁית (*ray-sheeth'*, "beginning") is linked to what follows. If that's the case, then Genesis 1:1 should read, "When God began to create the heaven and earth," rather than the traditional "In the beginning God created the heaven and the earth," a complete and finished event. If Alter is correct, then Genesis 1:1 marks the beginning of *a process that is still ongoing*. This opens up a profound and astonishing vision of creation. How does that affect our reading of the Bible, Genesis through Revelation?

— Chapter 5 —

Reading Exodus

Leon Kass writes that Exodus tells the story of the birth of a nation, a story that "sheds light on enduring questions about nation-building and peoplehood. It invites us to think about the moral meaning of communal life, the nature of political leadership, and the standards for judging a social order as better or worse."* It is also a riveting story filled with tension, drama, and intrigue—a terrific read on multiple levels!

1. At the end of Genesis, Jacob and his family of seventy settle in the land of Goshen, the very fertile northeastern region of the Nile River delta. When we turn the page to Exodus, four hundred years flash by and Jacob's family of seventy now numbers about _____.

Image: This image, taken from the International Space Station, illustrates the importance of the Nile River to Egypt. About 95 percent of Egypt's population lives within ten miles of the Nile River, the lifeblood of Egypt. *NASA*

* Leon Kass, *Founding God's Nation: Reading Exodus* (New Haven, CT: Yale University Press, 2021), 1–2.

2. If we date the exodus at 1446 BC, then the pharaoh Moses confronts is:

    □ Tutankhamun   □ Djoser

    □ Sneferu   □ Ramesses II

    □ Thutmose III

3. God brings the ten plagues on Egypt for three reasons. What are they?

    1. _____

    2. _____

    3. _____

4. Assuming the exodus occurred as reported in the Bible, draw on the map below the most probable route from Rameses to Mount Sinai, indicating where the Israelites would have crossed the Red Sea.

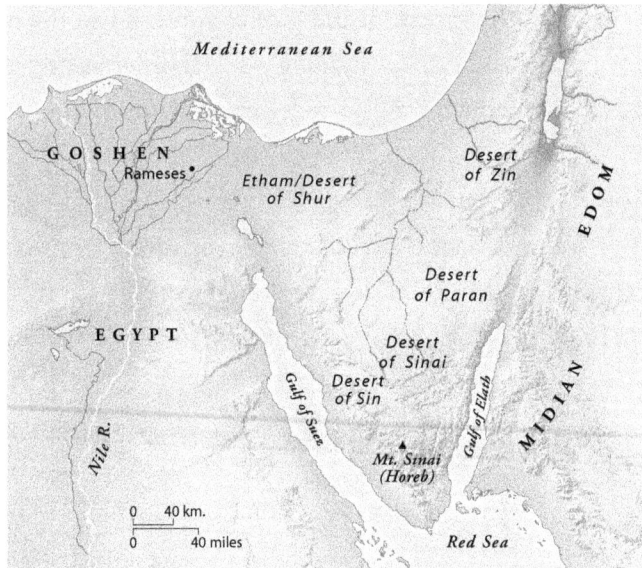

5. When God moves his people out of Egypt and into the Sinai wilderness, he reaffirms the covenant he made with Abram over half a millennium earlier, a covenant that involves _____ and _____.

6. In Exodus 20, God gives the Ten Commandments, ten principles by which a covenant people is to live with God and one another. The first four address their relationship with _____, while the last six address their relationship with _____.

7. After giving the Ten Commandments and demonstrating how to apply them, God offers his second great gift, the _____.

— Discussion Question —

Rabbi David Wolpe, one of the most influential rabbis in America and 2023–24 scholar in residence at Harvard Divinity School, proposes that the exodus did not take place as reported in the Bible. "Rather," he says, "the probability is, given the traditions, that there were some enslaved Israelites who left Egypt and joined up with their brethren in Canaan. This seems the likeliest scenario, a beautiful one that accords with the deeper currents of biblical tradition. The exodus was a very small-scale event with a large, world-changing trail of consequences." He goes on to say that "it is not the specifics of history that are central, but the theme of liberation and of God's providential care that is the theological center."[*]

Do you agree or disagree with Rabbi Wolpe? State the reasons for your position and present evidence to support it.

---

[*] David Wolpe, "Did the Exodus Really Happen?," Beliefnet, accessed September 24, 2024, https://www.beliefnet.com/faiths/judaism/2004/12/did-the-exodus-really-happen.aspx.

— Chapter 6 —

Reading Leviticus

In the literary structure of the Bible, Leviticus continues the book of Exodus, as Exodus continues the book of Genesis, suggesting that we study the three as one narrative unit. For Jews, Leviticus sits at the very heart of Torah, laying out two great pathways to a relationship with God: the first is the *approach* to God through *sacrifice*, and the second is the *walk* with God through *sanctification*. For Christians, when read through the lens of the epistle to the Hebrews, Leviticus offers a perfect portrait of the person and work of Christ.

1. When God reaffirms his covenant with Israel in Exodus 19, he gives his covenant people two great gifts: (1) the _____, God's comprehensive teaching on all aspects of human life, and (2) the _____, a physical structure by which a sinful people gain access to an infinitely holy God.

2. The theme of Leviticus is _____ and _____.

_____

Image: Model of the tabernacle. *GerthMedien*

3. The five great sacrifices offered at the tabernacle are:

    1. _____ offering
    2. _____ offering
    3. _____ offering
    4. _____ offering
    5. _____ offering

4. The formal study of the methodological principles of interpretation is called

    _____.

5. When the New Testament writers read the Hebrew Scriptures as foreshadowing Christ, this feature of Scripture is called _____.

6. When viewed through the lens of intertextuality, as the Israelites gained daily access to God through the repeated bloody sacrifices on the altar of burnt offering, so do we who are Christians gain access to God *once and for all* through the bloody sacrifice of _____.

— Discussion Questions —

1. I claim in *Reading the Bible* that if read through a Christian interpretive lens, Leviticus offers the most perfect picture of Christ in the entire Bible. Do you agree or disagree? State your reasons.

2. How do you understand the terms *clean* and *unclean* as used in Leviticus?

3. How might you apply lessons from the book of Leviticus in your own life? Give concrete examples.

For a superb in-depth study of Leviticus, check out Jacob Milgrom, *Leviticus: A Book of Ritual and Ethics*, A Continental Commentary (Minneapolis: Fortress, 2004).

— Chapter 7 —

Reading Numbers

After God delivers the Israelites out of Egypt, gives them the Ten Commandments at Mount Sinai, and instructs them in building the tabernacle and how to use it, in Numbers he gives instructions for counting the Israelites, organizing them by tribe, clan, and family, and positioning them around the tabernacle. Once organized, the Israelites then move out toward the promised land, a journey of roughly 150 miles . . . that takes forty years!

1. There are _____ Israelite men, ages twenty to fifty, in the Israelite camp.

2. The total population, including women, children, and men under twenty and over fifty is approximately _____.

3. Of that number, only _____ actually enter the promised land. Who are they? _____ and _____.

Image: Ana Maria Creasy/Logos Education Corp.

4. No sooner do the Israelites move out than they start complaining about the

   _____.

5. God provides _____ in the morning and _____ at night.

6. In the first two battles the Israelites fight, they defeat _____, king of the Amorites, and _____, king of Bashon.

7. In the hilarious story of Balaam and his talking ass, the famous prophet Balaam is from _____, near the _____ River.

8. _____, the king of _____, sent for Balaam.

9. Balaam attempts to curse the Israelites _____ times.

10. After attempting to curse the Israelites, Balaam, stung by his failure, immediately returns home, humiliated. True or false?

    ☐ True   ☐ False

Balaam and his talking ass (could be the peanuts Dr. C had in his pocket!). *Ana Maria Creasy/Logos Education Corp.*

— Discussion Question —

In Numbers 31 God commands Moses to attack the Midianites and kill every man. The Israelites do. But when Moses learns that his men have spared the Midianite women and children, he thunders, "Have you allowed all the women to live? . . . They were the ones who followed Balaam's advice and enticed the Israelites to be unfaithful to the LORD in the Peor incident, so that a plague struck the LORD's people. Now kill all the boys. And kill every woman who has slept with a man, but save for yourselves every girl who has never slept with a man" (31:15–18). This is deeply troubling on many levels. First, God orders Moses to slaughter every Midianite man, without exception, including the young boys. Second, Moses orders the extermination of every Midianite woman except those who are virgins. Moses' men may take the virgins for themselves.

One might argue that this is the God of the Old Testament speaking; the God of the New Testament is a God of love and would never say such a thing. Yet we read in Malachi 3:6—the book that transitions us into the New Testament—that God says, *"I the LORD do not change."* How might we understand this?

Chapter 8

Reading Deuteronomy

Deuteronomy is Moses' swan song. Moses dies at the end of Deuteronomy, and Israelite leadership passes to Joshua, who will lead the conquest of the promised land. But before Joshua does, Moses speaks his final words, bringing the Torah—the five books of Moses—to a close.

1. Moses gives his farewell address on the plains of _____.

2. Although we read "these are the words Moses spoke to all Israel in the wilderness east of the Jordan" (Deut. 1:1), it is clear that the "words Moses spoke" are the words of *the literary and theological portrayal* of Moses, not the words of Moses the *historical figure*; that is, they are the very *voice* of Moses, the _____, not the very *words* of Moses, the _____.

Image: The view Moses would have seen as he looked toward the promised land from the top of Mount Nebo. *Ana Maria Creasy/Logos Education Corp.*

3. On the plains of Moab, Moses does not address those who left Egypt during the exodus, for they have all died in the wilderness (except for Joshua and Caleb); rather, he addresses the _____.

4. Indeed, Moses includes *all* _____ by his choice of pronouns: *you, we, us, our, your,* and so on.

5. The core of the book of Deuteronomy is the scroll discovered in the temple at the time of king _____, over a thousand years after Moses dies.

— Discussion Question —

I have claimed that Scripture emerges from history, from real historical people, places, and events, but it is not *history* as we understand it in modern terms; rather, it is history reimagined, a poetic reconstruction to understand what the events *meant* in the context of forming a people's national self-identity. Understanding Scripture in this way by no means diminishes the story it presents, nor does it lessen the truth of God's Word; rather, it recognizes Scripture's complex textual history, and most importantly it recognizes the *literary* nature of the text.

Do you agree or disagree with this claim? Why?

Chapter 9

Reading Joshua, Judges, and Ruth

After Moses' death, Joshua leads the Israelites in their conquest of the promised land. As in the exodus the Red Sea had miraculously parted, allowing the Israelites to pass from Egypt to the Sinai on dry ground, so now the Jordan River miraculously stops flowing, allowing the Israelites to pass from the plains of Moab to begin their attack on Jericho. By the end of Joshua, the promised land is somewhat subdued, but there are still significant pockets of strong resistance.

Conquering the land is one thing; managing it is another. At this point, Israel is little more than a loose confederation of twelve tribes, a far cry from being a nation. When an outside threat appears, a leader emerges from the tribes to deal with the threat, and once the threat ends the leader returns to his farm and fields. At least that's the plan. But we all know that when people gain power and influence, they are loath to give it up. In total Israel has twelve judges, and after the first few, they become ever more corrupt, until we read at the end of Judges, "In those days Israel had no king; everyone did as they saw fit" (21:25). It was a time of moral, economic, and political collapse.

And then we turn to the book of Ruth. Ruth is a recapitulation into the time of

---

Image: ZU_09/iStock.com

the judges, a sparkling diamond in the muck and the mire of that era. Ruth is quite simply the greatest human love story in the entire Bible—and it is a milestone on our journey to the Messiah.

1. How many times do the Israelites march around Jericho before the "walls come tumblin' down?"
   ☐ three times ☐ thirteen times
   ☐ seven times ☐ eighteen times
   ☐ twelve times

2. When the priests carrying the _____ step into the Jordan River, the water _____.

3. When Joshua's spies enter Jericho on a reconnaissance mission, who hides them?
   ☐ Deborah ☐ Elizabeth
   ☐ Jael ☐ Ahoti
   ☐ Rahab

4. Of the twelve judges, only one of them is a woman. What is her name?
   ☐ Deborah ☐ Elizabeth
   ☐ Jael ☐ Ahoti
   ☐ Rahab

5. A judge is not a _____ but an ad hoc _____.

6. The last of the twelve judges is _____.

7. Who died with a tent peg through his skull?
   ☐ Heber ☐ Sisera
   ☐ Jabin ☐ Othniel
   ☐ Barak

8. What enabled Deborah to defeat the king of Hazor and his iron chariots?

9. Naomi is married to _____, and they have two sons, _____ and _____. They live in _____.

10. Boaz is Ruth's _____.

Ruth heads to Bethlehem with Naomi. Wood engraving by Julius Schnorr von Carolsfeld, published in 1860. *ZU_09/iStock.com*

— Discussion Question —

In the book of Joshua, we encounter God's command to put entire peoples "under the ban" (חרם, *cherem*), that is, to kill every living thing in Jericho: men, women, children, infants, and animals. Indeed, the Israelites are to do this with every city and village they attack in the promised land, the land of Canaan. Deuteronomy makes this command specific:

> When the LORD your God brings you into the land you are entering to possess and drives out before you many nations—the Hittites, Girgashites, Amorites, Canaanites, Perizzites, Hivites and Jebusites, seven nations larger and stronger than you—and when the LORD your God has delivered them over to you and you have defeated them, then you must destroy them totally. Make no treaty with them, and show them no mercy. Do not intermarry with them. Do not give your daughters to their sons or take their daughters for your sons, for they will turn your children away from following me to serve other gods, and the LORD's anger will burn against you and will quickly destroy you. (7:1–4)

This is even more extreme than Moses ordering the Israelites to kill all the people of Moab except for the young virgins (Num. 31:15–18).

Explore this issue of חרם (*cherem*) in depth, either in your own mind (you may want to research the term further and perhaps write an essay on the topic) or among your study group.

Chapter 10

Reading
The David Story

In *King David, the Real Life of the Man Who Ruled Israel*, Jonathan Kirsch observes:

At the heart of the Book of Samuel, where the story of David is first told, we find a work of genius that anticipates the romantic lyricism and tragic grandeur of Shakespeare, the political wile of Machiavelli, and the modern psychological insight of Freud. And, just as much as Shakespeare or Machiavelli or Freud, the frank depiction of David in the pages of the Bible has defined what it means to be a human being: King David is a symbol of the complexity and ambiguity of human experience itself.*

Image: Samuel anoints David as king (1 Samuel 16). Steel engraving by Raphael (Italian painter, 1483–1520) in the Loggia at the Vatican (Apostolic Palace), published in 1841. *ZU_09 /iStock.com*

---

* Jonathan Kirsch, *King David: The Real Life of the Man Who Ruled Israel* (New York: Ballantine Books, 2000), 1–2.

1. Consider what Jonathan Kirsch has to say about David in the previous quote. In what ways does David embody the "complexity and ambiguity of human experience itself"? In a single paragraph, write your thoughts about this in the space below.

2. In "Reading the David Story" in *Reading the Bible,* I spoke about reading the gaps in the David and Bathsheba incident of 2 Samuel 11:1–27. List three things you learned about "reading the gaps" in this story.

    1.

    2.

    3.

3. Why does David stay in Jerusalem when his men are fighting the Ammonites and besieging Rabbah?

4. What are David's motives for "taking" Bathsheba?

5. What are the implications of David's actions in this story?

— Discussion Question —

David is a magnificent warrior-king, a man to whom 73 of the 150 psalms are attributed, but he is also an outlaw, a murderer, an adulterer, and a very shrewd and brutal politician. So, why does God view David as "a man after his own heart" (1 Sam. 13:14), and why does God bring his own son, Jesus, through David's line? How do *you* view David?

Mediterranean
Sea

ISRAEL

Jerusalem• **BABYLONIAN**
JUDAH   **EMPIRE**

Euphrates R.

Tigris R.

•Babylon

0   200 km.

0   200 miles

— Chapter 11 —

Reading The Kings
of Israel and Judah

The united monarchy under kings Saul, David, and Solomon lasts only 120 years, from 1050–930 BC. With Solomon's death, his son Rehoboam becomes king and immediately triggers a civil war. The ten northern tribes become the nation of Israel, with its capital at Samaria under the leadership of Jeroboam, while the two southern tribes of Judah and Benjamin become the nation of Judah, with its capital at Jerusalem under the leadership of Rehoboam. From 930 BC through 586 BC, thirty-nine kings reign, nineteen in the north and twenty in the south. The northern kingdom of Israel falls to the Assyrians in 722 BC, while the southern kingdom of Judah falls to the Babylonians in 586 BC. The majority of the prophets operate during this time. The stories of these two kingdoms and their respective kings and prophets are some of the most riveting tales in the Bible, world-class literature of the highest order.

_____

Image: Judah's exile to Babylon

1. Both 1 and 2 Kings and 1 and 2 Chronicles tell the story of the kings of Israel and Judah, but they follow two very different narratives. Why? Check all that apply.

   ☐ 1 and 2 Kings are written during the Babylonian exile (586–539 BC), illustrating why the exile happened.

   ☐ 1 and 2 Kings are written as propaganda to highlight Judah's success.

   ☐ 1 and 2 Chronicles are written after the return from Babylon (post-539), seeking to inspire hope for the future.

   ☐ 1 and 2 Chronicles are poorly edited versions of 1 and 2 Kings.

   ☐ 1 and 2 Chronicles comprise an original composition written from a woman's point of view.

2. The two major *oral* prophets we meet in 1 and 2 Kings are _____ and _____.

3. Check off the "good" kings of Judah in the following list:

   ☐ Rehoboam   ☐ Ahaz

   ☐ Hezekiah   ☐ Manasseh

   ☐ Josiah

4. Check off the "good" kings of Israel in the following list:

   ☐ Ahab   ☐ Shallum

   ☐ Jehu   ☐ Zechariah

   ☐ Zimri

5. There are three major figures during the Old Testament period of the kings: _____, _____, and _____.

6. Of the three major figures, the _____ speaks to God on behalf of the people.

7. Of the three major figures, the _____ speaks to the people on behalf of God.

8. Of the three major figures, the _____ manages the affairs of state.

— Discussion Question —

In Old Testament times, every society had a king; indeed, it would be unthinkable to have any other form of government. God is Israel's king, but once God concedes kingship to a person, that person is to function in society as God's surrogate, leading God's people in the affairs of the world. If the king recognizes that reality, he does well, but this rarely happens. Of the thirty-nine kings of Israel and Judah, only five are good kings, and they're all from the southern kingdom of Judah.

Given that the three major figures in the Old Testament are the priest, the prophet, and the king, how would you increase the odds of having a good king?

— Chapter 12 —

Reading the Return from Captivity

The northern kingdom of Israel falls to the Assyrian Empire in 722 BC, and the population is deported into Assyria (northern Iraq of today), while the southern kingdom of Judah falls to the Babylonian Empire in 586 BC and their population is deported into Mesopotamia (southern Iraq and parts of Syria and Iran of today). Meanwhile, Cyrus inherits the Persian kingship from his father, Cambyses I, in 559 BC and begins expanding it eastward. On October 12, 539 BC, Cyrus enters Babylon, and Nabonidus, the Babylonian king who is staying in the city, surrenders to Cyrus without a fight. The Babylonian Empire thus ends, not with a bang but a whimper.

Cyrus is a very enlightened leader, however, and he issues a decree in 539 BC that allows all the people taken captive by Assyria and Babylon (not just the Jews) to return home and rebuild their cities, temples, and infrastructure. And Cyrus pays for it. The decree was issued on the clay cylinder pictured.

Image: Cyrus Cylinder (Akkadian cuneiform script on clay cylinder), 539 BC. © *2019 Zondervan, courtesy British Museum*

1. With Cyrus's decree, all the Jews in Assyria and Babylon joyfully return home. True or false?

    ☐ True   ☐ False

2. Once the Jewish returnees arrive in Jerusalem, they immediately begin rebuilding the temple. True or false?

    ☐ True   ☐ False

3. When the returnees finally complete rebuilding the temple, it is even more spectacular than the first temple that Solomon built. True or false?

    ☐ True   ☐ False

4. Once the Jews return to Jerusalem, they are warmly received by the now indigenous population. True or false?

    ☐ True   ☐ False

5. Both Ezra and Nehemiah display blatant xenophobia toward the current Jerusalem residents, forbidding the returning Jews from associating or mingling with any of them. True or false?

    ☐ True   ☐ False

— Discussion Questions —

1. Why do you think the vast majority of Jews living in the Persian Empire did not return to Jerusalem when they had the chance to do so?

2. Provide examples in Scripture of Jews who stayed in Persia and did not return.

3. Do you see any analogy between the Jews who returned to Jerusalem in 539 BC and those Jews who returned to the newly created state of Israel in 1948 after WWII?

Chapter 13

Reading the Poetical Books

The poetical books include Job, Psalms, Proverbs, Ecclesiastes, and the Song of Songs. Reading poetry is very different from reading historical narrative, so in this chapter we look closely at how each book operates as literature, and we develop the skills we need as readers to engage the texts as "educated readers" of Scripture.

1. In the linear narrative of Scripture, the book of Job is a recapitulation into the time of the patriarchs. True or false?

    ☐ True ☐ False

2. Job is a three-act drama, framed by a prologue and an epilogue, perhaps best viewed as a play on a stage. True or false?

    ☐ True ☐ False

Image: Solomon's Love Song. Wood engraving by Julius Schnorr von Carolsfeld, published in 1860. *ZU_09/iStock.com*

3. Of Job's three friends, Eliphaz is the voice of _____;
   Bildad is the voice of _____; and Zophar is the voice of
   _____.

4. The Psalms are songs meant to be sung, so if we are to understand them, we
   should examine them as _____.

5. English poetry for the most part employs rhyme and meter as its basic struc-
   tural elements, while Hebrew poetry uses _____ and
   _____.

6. _____ psalms are structured in the order of the Hebrew alphabet.

7. The prologue to the book of Proverbs reflects the literary genre of _____
   literature.

8. Individual proverbs are typically pithy sayings consisting of _____ lines,
   or versets.

9. The Hebrew title of Ecclesiastes is Qoheleth, meaning _____
   or _____.

10. Although the Song of Songs is often read in Judaism as a love song between God
    and Israel and in Christianity as a love song between Jesus and the church or the
    individual believer, the Song of Songs is frankly an _____.

— Discussion Questions —

1. What does Job learn in the book of Job? What do we learn?

2. What is your favorite psalm? Why?

3. Take a few minutes (or hours!) to write a two-verset proverb. Then share it with your study group, your friends, or your family.

4. What lesson(s) do we learn from Ecclesiastes?

5. Whom do you identify with in the Song of Songs? Who is your "beloved"?

Chapter 14

Reading the Major Prophets, Part 1

The Hebrew Bible, or Old Testament, features three main character roles: the king, the priest, and the prophet. The king leads God's people in the affairs of the world, ideally in consultation with God; the priest speaks to God on behalf of the people; and the prophet speaks to the people on behalf of God. Nearly always, the role of the prophet is confrontational, telling the king, the priests, and the people in no uncertain terms that they are straying far away from God. Consequently, prophets are typically despised, beaten, thrown in jail, run out of town, and sometimes killed.

There are two types of prophets: oral prophets and writing prophets. Oral prophets like Elijah and Elisha are great prophets, but they don't write a single word; writing prophets like Isaiah and Jeremiah write books. There are sixteen writing prophets: four major prophets and twelve minor prophets. Importantly, major prophets are "major" because their books are long; minor prophets are "minor" because their books are short. Isaiah has sixty-six chapters and Jeremiah has fifty-two, while Jonah has four chapters and Obadiah has one.

Image: Old Testament major prophets: Isaiah, Jeremiah, Ezekiel, Daniel. *mtcurado/iStock.com*

1. Prophets look down the long corridor of time to predict events in the distant future. True or false?

   ☐ True   ☐ False

2. A prophet always—100 percent of the time—speaks into their own _____ context.

3. Isaiah served as a prophet during the reigns of _____,
   _____, _____, and _____,
   740–686 BC.

4. Hezekiah faced a major crisis in 701 BC when _____, king of Assyria, attacks Jerusalem.

5. According to the vast majority of Old Testament biblical scholars the book of Isaiah was composed by at least three different authors over three distinct periods of time: the first includes chapters 1–39 and is called _____; the second includes chapters 40–55 and is called _____; and the third includes chapters 56–66 and is called _____.

6. If Isaiah is the "_____ prophet," then Jeremiah is the "_____ prophet."

7. In Isaiah 45 God calls _____ his "messiah."

8. Understanding events in New Testament times as being foreshadowed by events in Old Testament times is an example of _____.

9. _____ was the major prophet who witnesses the destruction of Jerusalem in 586 BC.

10. God tells which prophet not to marry?

☐ Isaiah   ☐ Ezekiel

☐ Jeremiah   ☐ Daniel

— Discussion Questions —

1. Anyone can claim to be a prophet (and there are plenty of false prophets in the Bible who do so!), so how can one know if a prophet is authentic? (Hint: See Deuteronomy 28:15–22).

2. All prophets speak (and write) within their own historical context—Isaiah during the events of 740–686 BC; Jeremiah during the events of 626–586 BC. What are the major conflicts and issues that each faced?

3. Are there prophets operating in today's world?

— Chapter 15 —

Reading the Major Prophets, Part 2

I t's difficult to find two prophets who differ more than Isaiah and Jeremiah ... until we encounter Ezekiel. While both Isaiah and Jeremiah may use strained rhetoric to deliver their messages and may even accompany it with graphic visual aids, Ezekiel is in a class by himself: he lies bound with ropes in a public park for months on end, wearing a sign, eating food cooked in an iron pan over poop; he digs holes in the walls of his house and crawls out through them, scampering off into the night; he takes flight on visionary journeys from Babylon to Jerusalem; he hears voices and peppers his prophecy with extravagant pornographic imagery. If Isaiah is the "thundering prophet" and Jeremiah is the "weeping prophet," then Ezekiel is—far and away—the "weird prophet." While Isaiah and Jeremiah operated in and around Jerusalem before it was sacked by the Babylonians in 586 BC, Ezekiel was taken to Babylon in 597 BC with the second wave of exiles (the first in 605 BC, the second in 597 BC, and the third in 586 BC). Ezekiel's entire public life as a prophet took place in Babylon.

Image: Ezekiel's vision at the epitaph of Edward Blemke, St. Mary's Basilica in Gdansk, Poland. *wjarek/stock.adobe.com*

Daniel offers an entirely different story. In the canon of the Jewish Bible (the Tanakh) Daniel is among the Ketuvim (the Writings), not among the Nevi'im (the Prophets). The Christian Old Testament canon moves Daniel to the Major Prophets, largely because Jesus believed Daniel to be a prophet (Matt. 24:15) and Jesus believed himself to be the "son of man" referenced in Daniel 7:13–14. From a literary perspective, we might view Daniel 1–6 as something of a historical novella, while Daniel 7–12 better fits the apocalyptic genre.

1. Immediately after God appoints Ezekiel as a prophet, Ezekiel springs into action—not with thundering words like Isaiah or with copious tears like Jeremiah, but with _____!

2. Ezekiel lies in a public park, bound with ropes and flinging stones at a model of Jerusalem for 390 days, wearing a sign that says _____.

3. He then turns over on his right side and wears a sign for forty days that says

   _____.

4. Ezekiel shaves his beard and his head bald and walks around as a sign of the total humiliation of the _____.

5. Ezekiel is the _____ of the prophets!

6. Daniel and his three friends are among Judah's royal family, and they are exiled to Babylon in 605 BC. Daniel's friends are Hananiah, Mishael, and Azariah; once in the Babylonian court, they are given Babylonian names: _____,
   _____, and _____.

7. After Daniel and his three friends learn the language and literature of the Babylonians, they enter King Nebuchadnezzar's service as _____
   and _____.

8. Daniel 1–6 tells the story of Daniel and his friends in the Babylonian court and the adventures they have, including Daniel interpreting _____ dream, the fiery _____, and Nebuchadnezzar's _____.

9. The stories in Daniel 1–6 are not based on historical reality; rather, they reflect the literary conventions of highly stylized oriental _____.

10. The second half of Daniel alludes to the bitter persecution of the Jews under Antiochus IV Epiphanes (c. 167–164 BC), the persecution that triggers the _____ revolt.

— Discussion Question —

Like Jeremiah, Ezekiel is both a priest and a prophet, although Ezekiel never served as a priest at the temple in Jerusalem because he was not yet thirty years old (the age a priest begins serving) when he was exiled to Babylon. Functioning as both a priest and a prophet requires two opposite tasks: The priest speaks to God on behalf of the people, while the prophet speaks to the people on behalf of God.

How might this conflict create cognitive dissonance in the priest-prophet? Give examples from the lives of both Jeremiah and Ezekiel.

Chapter 16

Reading the Minor Prophets, Part 1

The Assyrian Threat to Israel and Judah (732–612 BC)

AMOS, HOSEA, MICAH, AND JONAH

Since historical context is crucial in understanding the Prophets, I've abandoned the standard canonical order of the twelve Minor Prophets and instead grouped them chronologically into three sets: those who face the Assyrian threat to Israel and Judah (732–612 BC): Amos, Hosea, Micah, and Jonah; those who face the Babylonian threat to Judah (605–586 BC): Nahum, Zephaniah, Habakkuk, Joel, and Obadiah; and those who return from the Babylonian exile (539–410 BC): Haggai, Zechariah, and Malachi.

Image: Jonah and the big fish, bas relief by medieval artist Pellegrino da Sessa, also known as Peregrinus, thirteenth century. Cathedral of Sessa Aurunca, Campania, Italy. seraficus/iStock.com

1. Amos lives in _____, a small village in the southern kingdom of _____, and he works briefly in _____, in the northern kingdom of _____.

2. By occupation Amos is a _____ who also takes care of _____.

3. Amos confronts Amaziah, the priest of Bethel, and he tells Amaziah that the northern kingdom of Israel will go into _____, Amaziah's _____ and _____ will fall by the sword, and Amaziah's wife will become a _____ in the city.

4. God tells Hosea to marry Gomer, a _____.

5. Hosea's marriage to Gomer is a vivid allegory of _____ marriage to Israel.

6. Micah worked during the tumultuous years of Assyria's destruction of _____, and its invasion of Judah in 701 BC by the Assyrian king _____.

7. Micah operated at the same time as the great major prophet _____.

8. Jonah is not a collection of oracles like the prophets above; rather Jonah is a clever _____.

9. When the fish swallows Jonah, what does Jonah do while inside the fish? Check all that apply.
   - □ Jonah curses the fish.
   - □ Jonah meets Pinocchio.
   - □ Jonah writes a prayer.
   - □ Jonah curses God.
   - □ Jonah tries to eat his way out of the fish.

10. What is the primary lesson the book of Jonah teaches?

—— Discussion Question ——

For any thoughtful reader, the book of Hosea is deeply troubling. Why would God tell Hosea to marry a זנונים (*zaw-nim*), a "compulsive whore," and have children with her? Granted, the book of Hosea presents an allegory of God's "marriage" to Israel, who betrays God over and over again. But we must ask what is it like for Gomer to live with a man who is continually angry, a man who accuses her of chronic infidelity, a brooding man who insults her relentlessly, a man whom we might presume is physically violent with her.

As an instructive exercise, read Hosea from Gomer's point of view. How would the story change? How would your view of God change?

Chapter 17

Reading the Minor Prophets, Part 2

The Babylonian Threat to Judah (605–586 BC)

Nahum, Zephaniah, Habakkuk, Joel, and Obadiah

The Assyrian Empire (911–612 BC) was the largest and most powerful empire on the face of the earth in its day, an empire built by ruthless conquest. But like all empires, it fell, in its case to a coalition of Babylonians and Medes that destroyed its capital city of Nineveh in 612 BC and finished off Assyria at the battle of Carchemish in 605 BC. With that, the rising Babylonian Empire posed Judah's newest threat when Nebuchadnezzar attacked Jerusalem that same year and Judah became a reluctant vassal state to Babylon. Ultimately, Judah and Jerusalem fell to the Babylonians in 586 BC.

1. Nahum is a transitional prophet who speaks of the fall of _____ in 612 BC.

2. Nineveh is near modern-day _____, in Iraq.

3. _____ is a common expression in the Prophets used to introduce judgment and disaster.

4. The book of Zephaniah is written entirely in _____.

5. Zephaniah's twin themes are _____ and the _____.

6. Habakkuk is the prophet with a _____ for a brain.

7. In Habakkuk's view _____ and _____ have become totally corrupt, and God will use _____ to scourge his own people.

8. Joel uses the metaphor of _____ for the Babylonians' attack on Jerusalem.

9. _____ is the shortest book in the Bible.

10. Obadiah is an oracle against which nation?
    □ Babylon   □ Assyria
    □ Egypt   □ Moab
    □ Edom

— Discussion Questions —

1. If God uses Babylon to punish Judah and Jerusalem for their apostasy and corruption, would God possibly use another nation to punish us in our day?

2. Assyria totally destroyed Samaria in 722 BC and exiled its people throughout Assyria, while Babylon totally destroyed Jerusalem in 586 BC and exiled its people throughout Babylon. The exiles did not return until 539 BC under Cyrus the Great, king of Persia. What lesson was God teaching his people during that time?

Chapter 18

Reading the Minor Prophets, Part 3

Those Who Return from the Babylonian Exile (539–420 BC)

HAGGAI, ZECHARIAH, AND MALACHI

So far in the Minor Prophets we've addressed those who write during the Assyrian threat to Israel and Judah (740–609 BC): Amos, Hosea, Micah, and Jonah. And we've reviewed those who address the Babylonian threat to Judah (609–586 BC): Nahum, Zephaniah, Habakkuk, Joel, and Obadiah. We now move on to those prophets who address issues following the return from Babylonian exile (539–420 BC): Haggai, Zechariah, and Malachi.

1. Although Zerubbabel leads the people back to Judah after Cyrus the Great's decree of 539 BC, the kingdom of Judah is finished, the Davidic monarchy has ended, the temple is gone, and Jerusalem is little more than a pile of rubble. True or false?

   ☐ True   ☐ False

Image: The first of Zechariah's eight visions, ca. 1300, Sicily. *Public domain*

2. Although the Davidic monarchy will never be restored, Haggai envisions a Davidic dynasty in the _____.

3. Haggai enters our story in 520 BC. In 539 BC, thanks to Cyrus the Great, a Jewish contingent of exiles returns to Jerusalem and immediately begins to rebuild the temple. But due to local opposition, the work quickly stops. When Haggai arrives in 520 BC, he and Zechariah do what?
   □ File a law suit against those who are blocking the temple's construction
   □ Send a delegation to Cyrus, asking him to order the temple's completion
   □ Attack those who are blocking the construction
   □ Order the people to get to work . . . *now!*
   □ Form a prayer group to ask God for help

4. The book of Zechariah contains how many "visions"?
   □ three   □ twelve
   □ seven   □ forty
   □ eight

5. Zechariah is the _____ book among the twelve Minor Prophets.

6. Zechariah is famously the most _____ book among the Minor Prophets.

7. Zechariah's series of eight visions begins with that of a man on a red horse standing among a thatch of _____.

8. Seven of Zechariah's eight visions follow the same literary pattern: (1) what Zechariah _____; (2) Zechariah _____ what he sees; and (3) an angel _____ what Zechariah sees.

9. Malachi addresses his audience a few generations after that of Haggai and Zechariah, and he offers words of praise and thanksgiving, congratulating the people for their hard work and faithfulness in restoring the temple and Jerusalem. True or false?

   ☐ True   ☐ False

10. The "glory of the LORD"—the pillar of cloud and fire—that left the temple in Ezekiel 8–11 returns to the rebuilt temple in Malachi's day. True or false?

   ☐ True   ☐ False

— **Discussion Question** —

Because of Judah's apostasy, the Jews of Judah and Jerusalem are exiled to Babylon in 586 BC. Cyrus the Great, king of Persia, allows the Jews to return forty-seven years later in 539 BC. Only a small number do, however. The rest remain behind in what was then Persia.

Then 652 years later the Jews declare war on the Roman Empire, resulting in their catastrophic defeat in AD 73, the destruction of Jerusalem and the temple, and the expulsion of the Jews from their land once again. By the end of the Bar Kokhba revolt in AD 135, the Jews are scattered to the winds, not to return until 1,813 years later with the post-WWII creation of the modern state of Israel on May 14, 1948. The Jews once again return to their ancestral land, but not many do.

If you were a Jew in 539 BC or AD 1948, would you have returned? Why or why not?

THE NEW
TESTAMENT

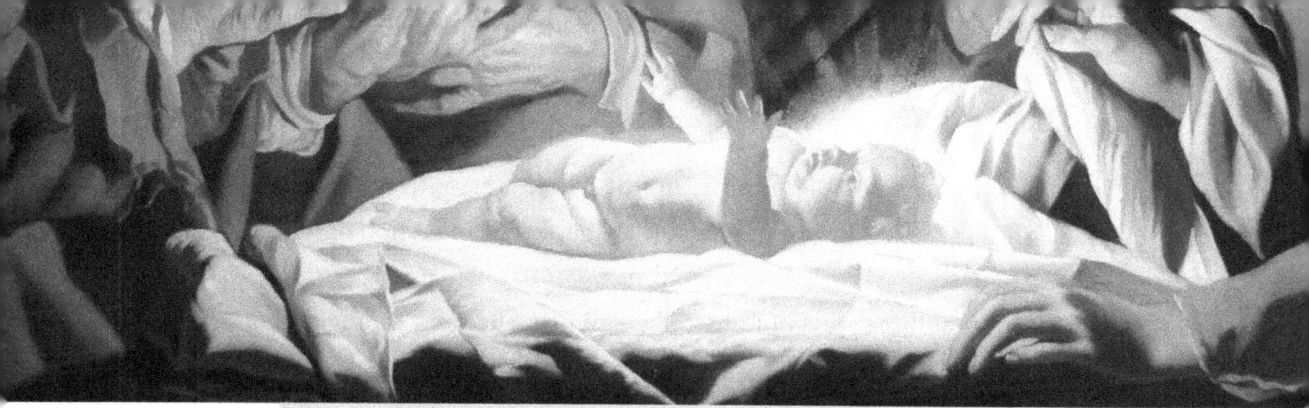

— Chapter 19 —

Reading the Gospel According to Matthew

Although not the first gospel written, Matthew's gospel sits at the head of the New Testament, functioning like a swinging door that links the Old and New Testaments together. Written by a Jew for a Jewish audience, Matthew begins with a three-part genealogy that moves from Abraham through David, David through the Babylonian exile, and the Babylonian exile through the birth of Jesus. In one deft movement, Matthew not only links the entire linear narrative of the Hebrew scriptures to the birth of Jesus, but he also identifies Jesus' birth as the culminating event in Israel's prophetic history.

1. Matthew designs his gospel with a chiastic structure and an underlying three-part christological foundation: (1) the _____ of Christ; (2) the _____ of Christ; and (3) the _____, _____, and _____ of Christ.

Image: Matthias Stom, *Adoration of the Shepherds* (oil on canvas), ca. 1650. *Public domain*

2. In addition, the name of Jesus envelops the whole, a narrative technique called _____, a word or phrase that "bookends" a section of text.

3. During the first three years of Jesus' public ministry, he went throughout Galilee _____, _____, and _____.

4. The Sermon on the Mount is an example of Jesus' _____.

5. The Sermon on the Mount is built on a four-part structure: (1) a nine-part clever and memorable _____, (2) six propositions that _____, (3) six concrete actions that _____ the law, and (4) a nine-part _____.

6. We might define Jesus' teaching as the _____ of a text, while Jesus' preaching is the _____ of a text.

7. Define what a parable does.

8. Give three examples of a parable in Matthew's gospel.

    1.

    2.

    3.

9. Now, let's turn from Jesus' teaching and preaching in Matthew to his healing and his power over both the natural and the supernatural, elevating him far above the mundane. Give three examples of Jesus' healing that are far beyond normal human ability.

   1.

   2.

   3.

10. The four gospels offer three examples of Jesus raising the dead. What are they?

   1.

   2.

   3.

— Discussion Question —

At the end of chapter 19 in *Reading the Bible,* I note that in Matthew's gospel Jesus follows the archetypical pattern of the hero's journey. How does Jesus differ from other classical heroes such as Gilgamesh, Homer's Achilles, Arjuna of the Hindu *Bhagavad Gita,* or even Frodo in J. R. R. Tolkien's *The Lord of the Rings?*

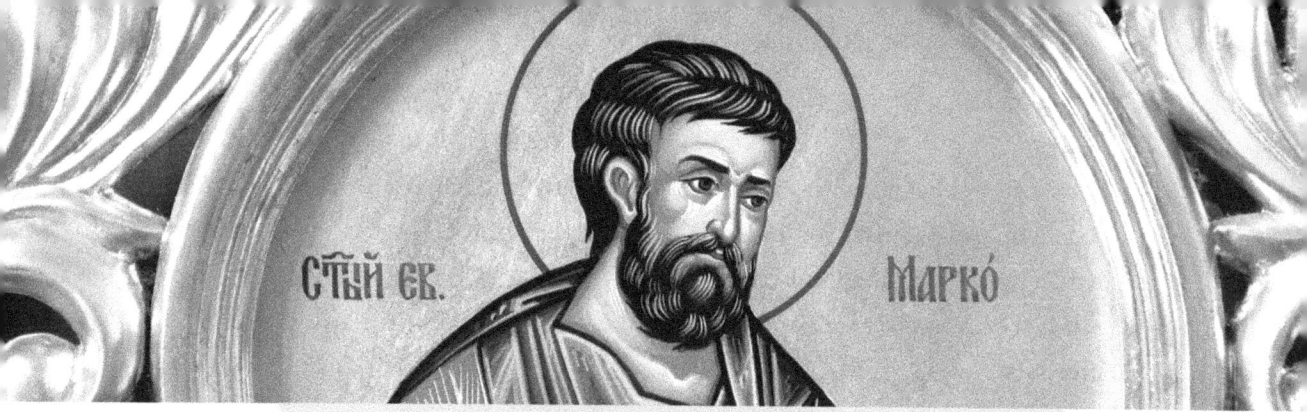

СТЫЙ ЕВ. МАРКО

Chapter 20

Reading the Gospel According to Mark

John Mark, the traditional author of the gospel of Mark, was not an apostle, but he was a young man on the fringes of the group that followed Jesus. He was a cousin of Barnabas, and he spent time in Rome with Peter. Mark probably wrote his gospel in the 60s, which makes it likely the first written gospel. It provides a radically different perspective from Matthew's gospel on the events that transpired during Jesus' public ministry. Matthew's gospel begins with a genealogy that starts with Abraham, leads through David, and brings us to Jesus, a smooth linear continuity, while Mark's narrative begins abruptly and rushes forward at breakneck speed, jolting to a sudden stop with the women at the tomb who did nothing, for they were terrified. As literary works, Matthew and Mark could not be more different.

1. Mark's prose style is to Matthew's as _____ is to
   _____.

Image: Icon of Saint Mark the Evangelist. Convent of the Holy Trinity in Lomnica. Vranov, Slovakia. *Adam Ján Figeľ/stock.adobe.com*

2. Mark's gospel begins with a sudden and dramatic proclamation: "*Beginning* the gospel of Jesus Christ, Son of God" (literal translation). The lack of a definite article preceding "Beginning" is called an _____ construction, and it serves to create an abrupt start, like a sudden thunderclap on a sunny afternoon.

3. Mark begins the prologue to his gospel with "Beginning the *gospel* of Jesus Christ" (1:1, literal translation), and he ends it with "repent and believe in the *gospel*" (1:15, literal translation). This fore and aft repetition of "gospel" is a framing device called an _____.

4. In Mark the intrusion of the gospel into daily life shocks and disorients those it touches, and they are _____.

5. In Mark, _____ and _____ precede the forgiveness of sins and point toward it; they do not accompany it or cause it.

6. In Mark violent action accompanies Jesus' baptism, as the heavens are _____ (not "opened") and the Holy Spirit descends _____ (not "on") him, and he is immediately _____ (not "led") into the wilderness, where he is tempted.

7. The word _____ runs through Mark's gospel like a thread of quicksilver. It occurs forty-one times, twenty-five with "and" in front of it, reinforcing the sense of urgency that drives the gospel.

— Discussion Question —

We could move verse-by-verse through Mark's gospel and highlight the literary devices he uses to create a sense of urgency and fear in his narrative. In contrast to

Matthew and Luke, Mark leaves us breathless! Why do you think Mark chose to deliver his gospel message in this way? If Mark was writing in the 60s, what was happening in the Roman Empire at that time—especially in Judah and Jerusalem—that would cause Mark to take this approach, one so very different from that of Matthew and Luke, the other two Synoptic Gospels?

— Chapter 21 —

Reading the Luke-Acts Narrative

The Gospel According to Luke and the Acts of the Apostles comprise a two-part narrative addressed not to a group of people but to a single man named Theophilus. Luke's purpose in writing Luke-Acts is so Theophilus "may know the certainty of the things [he has] been taught" (Luke 1:4), and Luke assures Theophilus that he has "carefully investigated everything from the beginning" (1:3) to assure that what he writes is correct. In Luke-Acts Luke takes us from Mary's annunciation through Jesus' death, burial, and resurrection, to the birth of the church forty days later at Pentecost, to Paul's arrival in Rome for his first trial in the early 60s.

1. How did Luke learn about Jesus? Check all that apply.
   - ☐ Reading Mark's gospel
   - ☐ Reading Matthew's gospel
   - ☐ Speaking with Paul
   - ☐ Meeting other apostles
   - ☐ Word of mouth

Image: Miguel Vaguer, *Saint Luke the Evangelist*, 1959. Iglesia El Buen Pastor, Valencia, Spain.
Renáta Sedmáková/stock.adobe.com

2. The name Theophilus means "loved by God," so it could refer to specific person, anyone who is loved by God (you or me?), the attorney who is to present Paul's defense at his trial in Rome, or someone else. What do you think?

3. Luke begins his gospel with a carefully structured single sentence arranged in a very symmetrical, balanced fashion. It is a beautiful example of classical Greek rhetoric . . . and then he never does it again. True or false?

   ☐ True   ☐ False

4. Luke then develops _____ for his _____ and the characters in his narrative.

5. Luke, unlike John in his gospel, gives Jesus the voice of _____.

6. In Mark the narrator _____ us about his characters; in Luke the narrator _____ us by allowing us to observe his characters in action.

7. After his resurrection, Jesus stays with his apostles for _____ days, teaching them what they need to know before he ascends into heaven. Then after _____ days, on the Jewish feast of Pentecost, the Holy Spirit arrives in Jerusalem.

8. As _____ was the driving force in the Gospels, so is the _____ the driving force in the Acts of the Apostles and onward.

9. Luke gives us a great deal of information about Jesus' mother Mary, more than any of the other gospels. Do you think Luke met Mary and spent time with her as he researched his gospel and Acts?

    ☐ Yes   ☐ No

Give support for your answer below.

10. In the overall structure of Luke-Acts, Luke begins with the whole Roman world and narrows down to Jerusalem and the cross; whereas, in Acts he begins with Jerusalem and the cross and expands outward to the whole Roman world. Thus, Luke-Acts has the shape of an hourglass. What are the implications of this structure for understanding the gospel message?

— Discussion Question —

We meet the Holy Spirit for the first time in Luke-Acts. What is the role of the Holy Spirit in the life of the church, both then and now? What is the role of the Holy Spirit in your own life?

Chapter 22

Reading the Gospel According to John

As a literary work, John's gospel stands shoulder to shoulder with the greatest works of ancient literature. In its finished form, it is a remarkably unified work with a simple narrative strategy and a deceptively simple prose style. Yet, of all the writings in the New Testament, John's gospel is the subtlest and most multilayered, moving us into profoundly intimate moments with Jesus and his disciples. In it we see Jesus through the eyes of an old man remembering precious moments from long ago, moments shaped through decades of reflection and recalled with a Proustian longing.

1. John's gospel operates outside of the _____ paradigm.

2. John begins his gospel with a _____, and he ends it with an _____; in between we follow Jesus and his disciples through _____ increasingly detailed cycles of Jewish festivals.

_____

Image: ZU_09/iStock.com

3. When John writes, "In the beginning was the Word, and the Word was with God, and the Word was God. . . . The Word became flesh and made his dwelling among us . . . full of grace and truth" (1:1, 14), he tells us that God Almighty, creator of heaven and earth, took on flesh and lived among us as a human being in the person of Jesus. True or false?

☐ True   ☐ False

John the Evangelist with his eagle symbol. Wood engraving, published in 1837. *ZU_09/iStock.com*

— Discussion Questions —

1. We witnessed the birth of John the Baptist and Jesus in Luke's gospel. Now in John's gospel, we bring the two together at the Jordan River and clarify their relationship, with John as the forerunner and Jesus as the Christ. When do you think both John and Jesus fully understood their identities and roles?

2. Why does Nicodemus come to Jesus at night?

3. What does Nicodemus learn in his meeting with Jesus?

4. In John's gospel we witness the aftermath of Peter denying that he knows Jesus. Put yourself in Peter's place and write below what you think Peter would say to Jesus if they sat down and talked.

5. Matthew, Mark, and Luke—the Synoptic Gospels—all draw on similar material and each other to craft their gospels, each writing for a particular audience. Why do you think John chose to do something so very different with his gospel?

6. Which of the four gospels is your favorite? Why?

Chapter 23

Reading Romans

Paul's epistle to the church at Rome—or Romans—is the most important of all Paul's epistles and letters, and for many Christians it is arguably the most important book in the entire Bible. We know from the Gospels and from church teaching that Jesus is the virgin-born, sinless Son of God who went to the cross on our behalf, who died, was buried, and was raised on the third day, enabling our salvation. That is who he is and what he did. In Romans Paul tells us how to reach out and *appropriate* who Christ is and what he did, how to move positionally from the world into the family of God.

1. Nearly all of Paul's epistles and letters are _____, addressing _____ in the communities to whom he is writing or to individuals to whom his letters are addressed.

2. Paul's epistles are meant to be delivered _____ to a community; whereas, Paul's letters are meant to be _____ by the person to whom they are addressed.

Image: Statue of Saint Paul, Vatican, Rome. *sedmak/iStock.com*

3. Paul writes his epistle to Rome to garner support for his planned fourth missionary journey to _____.

4. From a rhetorical perspective, the _____ brings the writer closer to his intended audience than an essay or other rhetorical form can do.

5. Paul structures his argument as a formal _____.

6. In this vivid form of argument a _____ challenges the writer's statements as he develops his argument, drawing the reader into an imaginary give-and-take conversation.

7. In Paul's day, Jewish commentary on the Torah was called _____.

8. Paul organizes Romans in an eight-part formal outline:
   - □ Introduction
   - □ Thesis statement
   - □ Demonstration by antithesis
   - □ Demonstration by example
   - □ Exposition of the thesis
   - □ Objections to the thesis
   - □ Practical implications of the thesis
   - □ Conclusion

   In this outline, where does Paul state clearly his main idea? Circle one of the above.

9. In Romans Paul views salvation in both _____ _____ and _____ terms.

10. In Paul's view, in the gospel the righteousness of God is revealed—a righteousness that is _____ from first to last.

sedmak/iStock.com

— **Discussion Questions** —

1. Paul argues in Romans that we are saved by grace through faith, an action that is profoundly personal. But once a person is "saved," what's next? How does one live out a "saved" life?

2. What is Paul's position on the Jews?

— Chapter 24 —

Reading Paul's Early Epistles

Galatians and 1 and 2 Thessalonians

— Galatians —

While Paul and Barnabas are on their first missionary journey (AD 46–48), Peter baptizes the Roman centurion Cornelius and his family, the first Gentile Christians, at Caesarea Maritima. This causes quite a stir with the Christian leaders in Jerusalem. At the same time, Gentiles are coming into the church in Syrian Antioch, the home church of Paul and Barnabas. A council is called in Jerusalem in AD 50 to address the issue, and the council decides that Gentiles are welcome in the church . . . *and they need not observe the Mosaic law*. Paul and Silas then launch the second missionary journey (AD 50–52) to deliver the council's message to the churches in Asia Minor.

Apparently, others from the Jerusalem Council objected to the decision, and they trail Paul and Silas, correcting the message Paul and Silas had delivered. When Paul reaches Corinth, he receives word from the churches in Galatia questioning what Paul

Image: Dr. Creasy and his intrepid students crossing the snowy mountains of Galatia (and tossing snowballs!). *Ana Maria Creasy/Logos Education Corp.*

had told them. Paul then fires off an epistle to the Galatian churches, calling them to task in no uncertain terms.

1. Paul writes a blistering epistle, saying in his opening statement that if anyone delivers a message contrary to Paul's, let that person _____.

2. Paul backs up his statement by invoking his _____.

3. Paul insists that in the church "there is neither _____ nor _____, neither _____ nor _____, nor is there _____ and _____, for you are all one in Christ Jesus" (Gal. 3:28).

— 1 and 2 Thessalonians —

4. When Paul and company reach Thessalonica, a church takes root, but Jewish opposition quickly arises and a mob chases Paul out of town after only _____. Paul makes his way to Corinth, and after several months Timothy and Silas finally arrive, bringing news (and perhaps a letter) from Thessalonica. Since Paul had spent only a brief time in Thessalonica, the believers understandably have many questions about their faith, which Paul had been unable to address when he was with them. _____ addresses those questions.

5. When Paul writes a letter or an epistle, he follows the rhetorical conventions of his day, conventions classified by Aristotle into three rhetorical categories:
   □ Deliberative: the art of persuading an audience to take (or not to take) an action
   □ Judicial: the art of justifying actions or beliefs, particularly in a court of law
   □ Epideictic: the art of praise or blame

Which does Paul use in 1 Thessalonians? Circle an answer above.

6. In 1 Thessalonians Paul had written about the Parousia—"the return of Christ"—and the great tribulation that would precede it. Apparently the Thessalonians had received word that the "return of Christ" had already happened, and consequently the persecution in Thessalonica had intensified. Paul wrote 2 Thessalonians in response, an epistle to refute the claim that Christ had already returned. Which rhetorical mode did Paul use to craft 2 Thessalonians?

☐ Deliberative: the art of persuading an audience to take (or not take) an action

☐ Judicial: the art of justifying actions or beliefs, particularly in a court of law

☐ Epideictic: the art of praise or blame

— Discussion Question —

When Paul begins writing Galatians and 1 and 2 Thessalonians, twenty years have not yet passed since Jesus' death, burial, and resurrection. Not a single word of the New Testament has yet been written. Christian theology and doctrine are just emerging in embryonic form. Paul plays a major role, of course, in defining the theological norms and doctrines that would later become normative. Yet, during this formative period of the church, competing ideas clashed, sometimes violently. It was a very tumultuous time. It wouldn't be until AD 325 at the Council of Nicaea that the fundamental beliefs of the church would be clearly defined and articulated.

How do you understand this process of clarifying our basic Christian beliefs? Who are the major players? Is Christian doctrine still evolving today?

Chapter 25

Reading Paul's Corinthian Correspondence

O f all the churches Paul founded, the Corinthian church posed the greatest challenges, both during its foundation and as it developed during Paul's lifetime. In AD 50 the city of Corinth was not only an exceedingly prosperous double seaport town, but it was the political and economic capital of Achaia. Because of its vibrant maritime trade, Corinth hosted a large transient population from the many cultures that surrounded the Mediterranean, and as one would expect, those cultures exerted significant social, religious, political, and economic influences on the resident population. In Corinth, temples of Aphrodite, Apollo, Poseidon, Hermes, Asclepius, and Isis coexisted with a Jewish synagogue and with the embryonic Christian "house" churches, posing significant challenges for the developing Christian community.

Image: Dr. Creasy and his students inspect the Erastus inscription in Corinth. *Ana Maria Creasy/ Logos Education Corp.*

1. Although the Bible includes two epistles to the Corinthians, the Corinthian correspondence consists of at least _____ exchanges between Paul and the church.

2. In addition to the household of Stephanas, Paul baptized only two men in Corinth: _____ and _____.

3. Paul meets a married couple from Rome who had a tentmaking shop in Corinth: _____ and _____.

4. Why was the married couple in question #3 in Corinth?
   - ☐ That's where their extended family lived.
   - ☐ There was a huge demand for tents in Corinth.
   - ☐ They were setting up a tentmaking franchise in Corinth.
   - ☐ They had been exiled from Rome by the emperor Claudius.
   - ☐ They were in transit to Alexandria to open another shop there.

5. When Paul was ejected from the Corinthian synagogue, where did he go?
   - ☐ Back to the tentmaking shop
   - ☐ Next door to the home of Titus Justus
   - ☐ To Ephesus, where he'd have his greatest success
   - ☐ To the local *popina* to have lunch
   - ☐ To the local jail

6. The leader of Corinth's synagogue, _____, takes Paul to court. His case is presented to the learned and distinguished judge, _____, who rightly refuses to hear the case since it does not involve a civil or criminal misdemeanor or felony.

7. Knowing that he faces great difficulties and dangers in Corinth, Paul takes a _____ vow and continues his work, spending a full _____ months in Corinth.

8. When Paul is in Ephesus (AD 54–57), he learns that the Corinthian church faces serious difficulties. Check all that apply:
   □ Factions and divisions are splitting the church.
   □ Members of the Corinthian synagogue have successfully sued the church and shut it down.
   □ There is rampant sexual immorality.
   □ The Roman emperor has expelled the Christians from Corinth.
   □ Corinthian church members are suing each other in court.

9. First Corinthians is first and foremost a love letter to the Corinthian church. True or false?
   □ True   □ False

10. Second Corinthians is actually Paul's _____ correspondence with the Corinthian church, and in it he seeks to _____ those in the church.

11. The world of the Bible is very different from the world we live in. Although the world of the Bible differs in degree between the Old and New Testaments, in general the world of the Bible is:
   □ _____
   □ _____
   □ _____
   □ _____

— Discussion Questions —

1. After reading the Corinthian correspondence, do you see any similarities between the Corinthian church and today's churches?

2. Paul is a missionary, not a pastor. How do the two roles differ?

3. In today's world many people are "church planters," founders of church communities. Once "planted," should the founder of a church community continue with that community for life, or should the founder stabilize the community and then move on? What are the advantages and disadvantages of each option?

— Chapter 26 —

Reading Paul's Prison Epistles

Ephesians, Philippians, Colossians, and Philemon

After Paul's arrest in Jerusalem in AD 54, he is transferred to Caesarea Maritima, not as a prisoner but as a Roman citizen under protective custody. Paul did not commit any offense under Roman law, and the Jewish leadership in Jerusalem had vowed to assassinate him. He spends two years in Caesarea Maritima at the administrative complex and home of Governor Antonius Felix, the Roman procurator (AD 52–58), while Felix sorts out Paul's legal issues. During this time, Paul often has friendly conversations with Felix and his Jewish wife, Drusilla.

When Felix's term as governor ends in AD 58, Porcius Festus (c. 59–62) replaces him, and Festus correctly goes up to Jerusalem to meet with his constituency, the Jewish leadership, who demands that Paul be handed over to them. Returning to Caesarea Maritima, Felix asks Paul if he is willing to go. Paul gives an

---

Image: Dr. C. and his students at the raw archaeological site of Colossae, home of Philemon. *Ana Maria Creasy/Logos Education Corp.*

emphatic "No!" and exercises his right as a Roman citizen to appeal his case directly to Rome. So, to Rome Paul goes, not as a prisoner, but as a Roman citizen exercising his legal right of appeal. Once in Rome, Paul spends two years "in his own rented house" (Acts 28:30) with a Roman guard to protect him. Paul's "chains" are his legal issues keeping him in Rome, not physical chains, for it was illegal to chain a Roman citizen (Acts 22:29).

— Ephesians —

1. Ephesians offers a dazzling display of rhetorical fireworks, written in a highly ornamented _____ or _____ style, the second sentence consisting of _____ words in Greek, with multiple levels of _____.

2. Paul probably wrote Ephesians as a _____ or _____ to be read or preached at many different church communities in Asia Minor, since "in Ephesus" is not present in any Ephesian manuscripts until the fifth century AD.

3. Ephesians needs to be _____ in order to be understood and rightly appreciated.

— Philippians —

4. On his second missionary journey, Paul and his companions arrive in Philippi, and he meets _____ and her friends down by the _____ River, where he baptizes them. Paul and his companions then stay at Lydia's home, and a small church community forms.

5. In Philippi, Paul and Silas end up being flogged, chained, and jailed. While they are in jail, an earthquake strikes, the jailer thinks his prisoners have escaped, and he is about to kill himself. In the end, Paul _____ the jailer and _____, and because Paul—a Roman citizen—has been flogged and chained, he weasels an apology out of the _____ and is politely escorted out of town.

— Colossians —

6. Paul had never visited Colossae. True or false?

   ☐ True   ☐ False

7. Ephesians and Colossians are closely linked in both in content and style. True or false?

   ☐ True   ☐ False

8. The Colossians were experiencing misleading teaching similar to that in the Galatian territory. True or false?

   ☐ True   ☐ False

— Philemon —

9. Paul writes to Philemon, the leader of the church in Colossae, encouraging him to take back his escaped slave, _____, no longer as a slave, but now as a Christian brother.

10. Paul's short letter—only 336 Greek words—is a masterpiece of _____ arm-twisting.

— Discussion Questions —

1. When Paul wrote Romans in AD 57, he sought to create a home base from which to launch his fourth missionary journey to Spain. Now that Paul was stuck in Rome for two years (AD 60–62), how do you imagine he may have continued building that home base?

2. We leave the Acts of the Apostles with Paul in Rome, living "in his own rented house" and welcoming all who came to see him (Acts 28:30). We hear no more of Paul after Acts 28. We know that Paul was martyred in Rome during the persecution under Nero, AD 64–68, along with Peter and many others. In your discussion group (or by writing a short story), fill in those years between AD 64 and 68. What do you think happened to Paul?

Chapter 27

Reading Paul's Pastoral Letters

1 and 2 Timothy and Titus

Paul worked tirelessly for more than two decades, evangelizing throughout Asia Minor and the Mediterranean world, but he didn't do it alone. Among his many traveling companions were Barnabas, Silas, Timothy, Titus, Mark, Erastus, Aristarchus, Gaius, Trophimus, Tychicus, Priscilla, Aquila, and Luke, along with many others who played local roles. Although Paul had close relationships with many of his companions, no relationship was closer than the one he had with Timothy, whom he considered his son. Timothy was a young man from Lystra, a city in central Anatolia about nineteen miles southwest of Iconium. Today Lystra is the small Turkish village of Gökyurt, with a population of fewer than one hundred people.

Image: The Lycian Way in southwestern Turkey. *rheins/CC BY 3.0*

— 1 and 2 Timothy —

1. Paul's pastoral letters to Timothy and Titus are _____, meant to be read privately, that address specific problems in their current work.

2. In 1 Timothy Paul gives Timothy advice on correcting immediate problems in a specific community, in this case _____. He is not writing _____ or _____.

3. Paul writes 1 Timothy in the rhetorical form of _____, a style of exhortation urging his audience to continue down its original path, and he does so through a series of imperatives or commands.

4. In 1 Timothy Paul presents himself as _____, issuing a checklist of tasks for Timothy to accomplish.

5. The main problem Paul sees in the Ephesian leadership is teachers who promote _____.

6. When Paul writes 2 Timothy, Paul is on "death row" in Rome (c. AD 64–68), and we might consider this letter his last _____.

7. Unlike the commanding tone of 1 Timothy, the tone of 2 Timothy is _____ _____.

— Titus —

8. Unlike Timothy, Titus stands in the shadows of Scripture, a hardworking, unsung hero, present in _____, one of Paul's earliest epistles; in

_____, one of Paul's middle epistles; and at the very end, in the letter addressed to him, _____.

9. Paul chooses Titus to finish up the work on the newly formed churches in _____ during the mid-60s.

10. Paul did not like the island of Crete or the people who lived there. Following his first brief visit to Crete, he was shipwrecked on Malta and bitten by a viper en route to Rome, and on this visit he can't wait to leave, quoting the Cretan philosopher-poet Epimenides: _____
_____ (1:12)!

— Discussion Question —

This brings us to the conclusion of Paul's epistles and letters. We've studied the Acts of the Apostles and Paul's transition from sinner to saint, from being the greatest persecutor of the church to being its greatest defender. In the pantheon of the heroes of the faith, Paul sits at the very summit.

In your discussion group (or in a personal essay) summarize Paul's contribution to our understanding of Jesus and his church.

Chapter 28

Reading the General Epistles and Letters

Hebrews; James; 1 and 2 Peter;
1, 2, and 3 John; Jude

The General Epistles and Letters is a catch-all category for the remaining epistles and letters of the New Testament. Hebrews is perhaps the most complex book in the New Testament, and from a Christian perspective it functions as something of a gloss on the book of Leviticus. James is "the brother of the Lord," the leader of the church in Jerusalem, and the red-headed Dutch uncle of Scripture who offers sound, practical advice for living the Christian life. Peter's epistles offer his last thoughts on Jesus before his own crucifixion, emphasizing in 2 Peter that he was an eyewitness to Jesus' life, death, and resurrection, and noting that he, along with James and John, was present at Jesus' transfiguration and witnessed Jesus' divinity revealed. John's one epistle and two letters continue the dichotomy of light/dark, love/hate that we find in his gospel, as well as his strong condemnation of false teachers. And the little book

Image: Engraving of Abraham meeting Melchizedek, 1859. Biblische Geschichte des alten und neuen Testaments, Germany. *Zdenek Sasek/stock.adobe.com*

of Jude offers additional condemnation of false teachers while encouraging believers to build themselves up in their most holy faith, pray, and stay rooted in their love of God as they await the Lord's mercy and their entrance into eternal life.

— Hebrews —

1. Who wrote Hebrews?

   ☐ Paul

   ☐ Apollos

   ☐ Luke

   ☐ Philo of Alexandria

   ☐ Don't have a clue

2. Hebrews 7 views Melchizedek as an archetype of _____.

3. Hebrews might be best understood as a _____ that _____ the inspired text of the Old Testament, shows its _____ for the present, and urges its hearers to obey its _____.

— James —

4. Which James wrote the epistle of James?

   ☐ James, son of Zebedee

   ☐ James, son of Alphaeus

   ☐ James, the "brother of the Lord"

   ☐ James, father of the apostle Judas (not Judas Iscariot)

   ☐ James whose mother was Mary

5. James offers good _____ from one who understands doubt, weakness, the resolve to correct one's behavior, and striving heroically to live a life consistent with one's faith in Christ.

— 1 and 2 Peter —

6. Peter addresses his first epistle to the Christian communities in five provinces of Asia Minor: _____, _____, _____, _____, and _____.

7. Who helped Peter write 1 Peter?
   - ☐ Peter's wife
   - ☐ Silas
   - ☐ John
   - ☐ Timothy
   - ☐ Paul

8. Second Peter is an urgent message written by Peter himself as he sits on "death row" in the Mamertine prison in Rome. In this epistle Peter urges believers to be rooted in sound _____, to persevere in the face of _____, and to hold fast to the _____.

— 1, 2, and 3 John —

9. In 1 John the apostle vehemently defends his understanding of Christ, insisting upon it, and demanding that those who teach otherwise be _____ from the community and _____ permitted to hold leadership positions; whereas, 2 and 3 John are very short letters, the second addressed to _____ and the third addressed to _____.

— Jude —

10. Jude is a very brief epistle of only twenty-five verses that, like 1 John, addresses _____, "certain individuals whose condemnation was written about long ago" (Jude 4).

— Discussion Question —

Melchizedek is an enigmatic figure in Scripture. He appears out of nowhere in Genesis 14, Abraham gives him a tenth of the plunder he has taken from the kings who kidnapped Lot and his family, Melchizedek blesses Abraham, and then Melchizedek disappears from Scripture until Hebrews 7.

What do you make of this figure? Who is he? And where did he come from? How does he fit into the linear narrative of Scripture?

— Chapter 29 —

Reading Revelation

Revelation emerges from the chaotic second half of the first century AD Roman Empire, a tumultuous time politically, economically, culturally, and religiously. Fifty years see eight emperors: Claudius, Nero, Galba, Otho, Vitellius, Vespasian, Titus, and Domitian, seven of whom meet violent deaths. A persecuted minority within the Roman Empire, the emerging church becomes the target of two state-sponsored persecutions, one under Nero and the other under Domitian. Rome burns twice. Jerusalem and the temple are destroyed in AD 70, bringing one thousand years of temple worship to an abrupt end. Vesuvius erupts in AD 79, spewing volcanic ash across the entire Mediterranean world, and the last eyewitnesses of Jesus' public ministry begin dying out. In the Olivet Discourse, Jesus had spoken of a time of great tribulation and of "the Son of Man coming on the clouds of heaven, with power and great glory," and he added, "this generation will certainly not pass away until all these things have happened" (Matt. 24:21, 30, 34). In the second half of the first century, it seemed to the Christian community that the end Jesus had spoken of was at hand and his return in glory was imminent. That's the context for the book of Revelation.

Image: Mosaic depicting Saint John dictating to his scribe on the isle of Patmos. *johncopland/iStock .com*

1. The book of Revelation is a tightly woven apocalyptic vision that presents the death throes of _____, the triumphant return of _____, the climactic battle between _____, the last _____, and the birth of a _____ and a _____.

2. John builds his narrative on a framework of sets of _____ and _____, prime numbers, complete and indivisible.

3. The basic structure of Revelation is thus tripartite: (1) _____ (chap. 1); (2) _____ (chaps. 2–3); and (3) _____ (chaps. 4–22).

4. The Greek word translated "Revelation" is ἀποκάλυψις (*ap-ok-al'-oop-sis*), meaning _____.

5. There are close parallels between the book of Revelation and _____.

6. In Revelation, John sees a dazzling figure behind him holding seven lampstands and seven stars. The lampstands are seven _____, and the seven stars are the churches' seven _____.

7. What churches are *not* among the seven churches in Revelation?
   - ☐ Ephesus
   - ☐ Pisidian Antioch
   - ☐ Colossae
   - ☐ Smyrna
   - ☐ Philadelphia
   - ☐ Pergamum
   - ☐ Thyatira
   - ☐ Iconium
   - ☐ Laodicea
   - ☐ Sardis

8. What is Revelation's literary genre?

9. Where did John write the book of Revelation?

10. If we understand the Bible as a unified literary work, we begin our story of humanity in the _____ of Genesis 2 and we end our story in the _____ of Revelation 22.

— Discussion Questions —

1. We understand from our reading of the Prophets that a prophet *always* speaks into his own historical context. As we move into the second, third, and fourth centuries, the events described in Revelation didn't take place, which was a serious impediment to its inclusion in the Christian canon. That being the case, how might we best understand Revelation today?

2. There are those since the late nineteenth century through today who understand Revelation as long-range, predictive prophecy, as events that will play out exactly as described in Revelation in a future yet to come. What are the strengths of this position? What are its weaknesses?

Answer Key

Chapter 1: Four Foundational Principles

1. geography, history, unified literary work, Word of God
2. and 3.

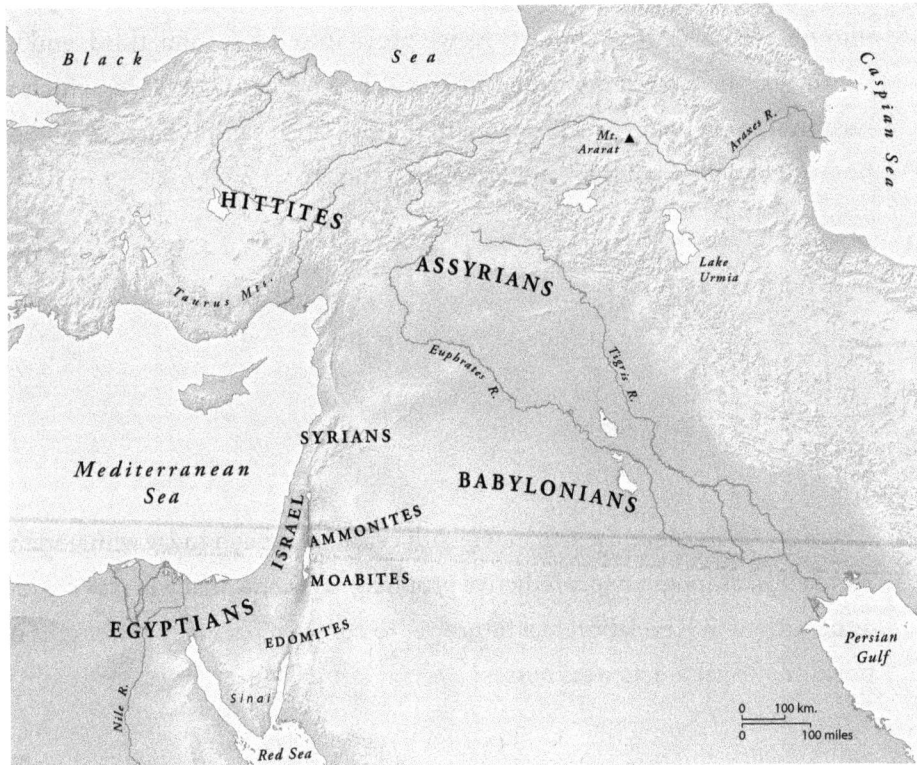

4.

5. Sea of Galilee, Dead Sea, Jordan River

6. Egyptian, Assyrian, Babylonian, Persian, Roman

7. Roman

8. Genesis, Revelation, linear, recapitulation

Chapter 2: Writing the Bible

1. traditional, form-critical

2. Matthew, Mark, Peter, researched

3. form-critical, narrative, redaction, feminist, postcolonial, rhetorical, literary

4. oral

5. evolves or changes

Chapter 3: The Canon of Scripture

1. measuring rod, standard

2. Mesopotamia, Egypt

3. scribes

4. literary

5. consensus

6. pseudepigrapha

7. The Hebrew scriptures being translated into Greek for Ptolemy's great library at Alexandria, Egypt. The translation became known as the Septuagint (or the LXX), for the seventy-two Jewish scholars who completed the translation. Only the Torah, or the five books of Moses (Genesis, Exodus, Leviticus, Numbers, and Deuteronomy), were included. Over time other books were added to it.

8. The Dead Sea Scrolls offer clear evidence of a Hebrew canon still in flux during Jesus' day. They also validate the integrity of the Old Testament texts, for they are nearly identical to Old Testament texts from a thousand years later.

9. true

10. AD 393 at the Council of Hippo

11. Jerome's Latin Vulgate

12. Apocrypha or deuterocanonical books

Chapter 4: Reading Genesis

1. mythopoeic

2. Abraham and Isaac (12:1–25:18), Isaac and Jacob (25:19–36:43), Jacob and Joseph (37:1–50:26)

3. creation/birth, in a coffin in Egypt/death

4. ambiguity

5. nothing

6. Joseph was a teenager when he went missing. His brothers have no idea what happened to him. Joseph is now a grown man with a family in Egypt. He is bathed and clean-shaven like all Egyptian men are (and Hebrews are not). He speaks Egyptian. He is the grand vizier of Egypt, second only to Pharaoh. There are no dots to connect.

7. Judah

8. Of Jacob's twelve sons, it is Judah, the most unlikely of them all, who is the forerunner of Jesus.

Chapter 5: Reading Exodus

1. two million

2. Thutmose III

3. to demonstrate to the Israelites who God is, to demonstrate to the Egyptians who God is, to bring judgment on the gods of Egypt

4.

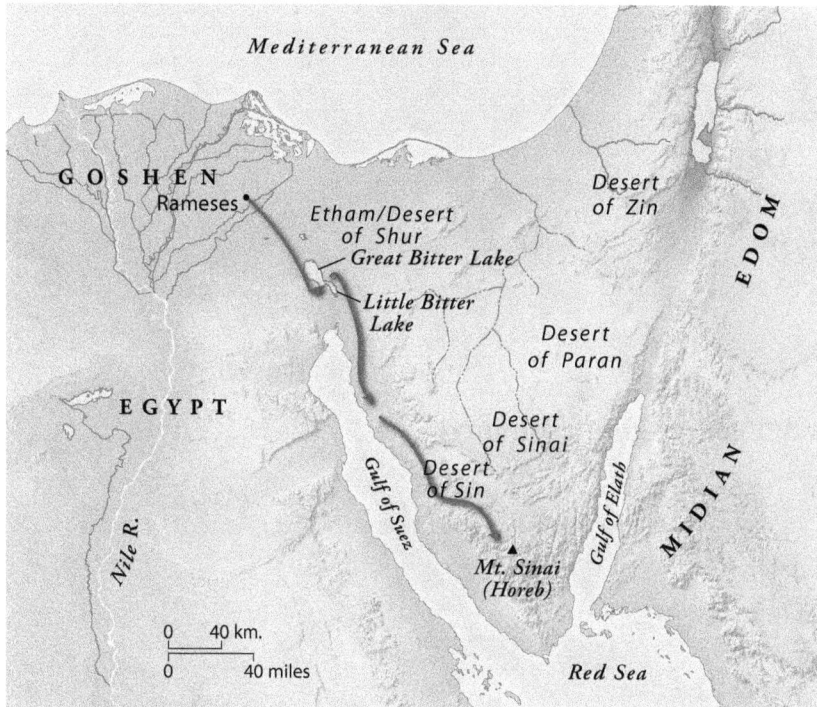

5. progeny, property

6. God, one another or the community

7. tabernacle

Chapter 6: Reading Leviticus

1. Law, tabernacle

2. sacrifice, sanctification

3. sin, guilt, burnt, grain, peace/fellowship

4. hermeneutics

5. intertextuality

6. Christ on the cross

Chapter 7: Reading Numbers

1. 603,550
2. two million
3. two, Joshua, Caleb
4. food
5. manna, quail/meat
6. Sihon, Og
7. Pethor, Euphrates
8. Balak, Moab
9. three
10. false

Chapter 8: Reading Deuteronomy

1. Moab
2. *ipsissima vox, ipsissima verba*
3. new generation
4. future generations
5. Josiah

Chapter 9: Reading Joshua, Judges, and Ruth

1. thirteen
2. ark of the covenant, stops flowing
3. Rahab
4. Deborah
5. judicial figure, military leader
6. Samson
7. Sisera
8. A heavy rain floods the Kishon River, turning the Jezreel Valley into mud and making Jabin's iron chariots worthless.
9. Elimelek, Mahlon, Kilion, Bethlehem
10. kinsman-redeemer

Chapter 10: Reading the David Story
All of the questions in this lesson are open-ended.

Chapter 11: Reading the Kings of Israel and Judah
1. 1 and 2 Kings are written during the Babylonian exile (586–539 BC), illustrating why the exile happened. 1 and 2 Chronicles are written after the return from Babylon (post-539 BC), seeking to inspire hope for the future.
2. Elijah, Elisha
3. Hezekiah, Josiah
4. There are none.
5. priest, prophet, king
6. priest
7. prophet
8. king

Chapter 12: Reading the Return from Captivity
1. false
2. true
3. false
4. false
5. true

Chapter 13: Reading the Poetical Books
1. true
2. true
3. experience, tradition, religion
4. lyric poetry
5. parallelism, stressed syllables
6. Acrostic
7. advice to a son
8. two

9. teacher, preacher
10. erotic love poem

Chapter 14: Reading the Major Prophets, Part 1

1. false
2. historical
3. Uzziah, Jotham, Ahaz, Hezekiah
4. Sennacherib
5. Proto (First)-Isaiah, Deutero (Second)-Isaiah, Trito (Third)-Isaiah
6. thundering, weeping
7. Cyrus, king of Persia
8. intertextuality
9. Jeremiah
10. Jeremiah

Chapter 15: Reading the Major Prophets, Part 2

1. street theater
2. sin of the House of Israel
3. sin of the House of Judah
4. Jewish people
5. P. T. Barnum
6. Shadrach, Meshach, Abednego
7. translators, interpreters
8. Nebuchadnezzar's, furnace, madness
9. folktales
10. Maccabean

Chapter 16: Reading the Minor Prophets, Part 1

1. Tekoa, Judah, Bethel, Israel
2. shepherd, sycamore-fig trees
3. captivity, sons, daughters, prostitute

4. whore
5. God's
6. Samaria, Sennacherib
7. Isaiah
8. short story
9. Jonah writes a prayer
10. open-ended question

Chapter 17: Reading the Minor Prophets, Part 2

1. Nineveh
2. Mosel
3. "Woe"
4. poetry
5. universal judgment, day of the Lord
6. question mark
7. Judah, Jerusalem, the Babylonians
8. a locust swarm
9. Obadiah
10. Edom

Chapter 18: Reading the Minor Prophets, Part 3

1. true
2. eschatological future
3. Order the people to get to work . . . *now*!
4. eight
5. longest
6. obscure
7. myrtle trees
8. sees, questions, interprets
9. false
10. false

Chapter 19: Reading the Gospel According to Matthew

1. person; proclamation; suffering, death, resurrection
2. inclusio
3. teaching, preaching, healing
4. teaching
5. introduction, exceed the law, implement, call to action
6. explication, application
7. A parable is a clever story that illuminates a common, ordinary truth in a striking and memorable fashion.
8. The parable of the vineyard workers (10:1–16); soils (13:1–23); wheat and tares (13:24–30); mustard seed (13:31–32); leaven (13:33); hidden treasure (13:44); pearl of great price (13:45–46).
9. Healing a leper (8:1–4); healing the Centuran's servant (8:5–13); healing Peter's mother-in-law (8:14–15); healing a paralized man let down through Peter's roof (9:1–8); Healing a man with a withered hand on the Sabbath (12:9–14); healing a bleeding woman (9:20–22); raising Jairus's daughter (9:18, 23–26); 27–31); heals two blind men (9:27–31); heals a mute man (9:32–34); heals the blind, mute demoniac (12:22–23); heals the sick at Gennesaret that touch his garment (14:34–36); heals a Gentile woman's daughter (15:32–39); heals boy with an unclean spirit (17:14–20); heals blind Bartimaeus at Jericho (20:29–34).
10. Jesus raises Jairus's daughter (Matthew 9:18, 23–26; Mark 5:21–24, 35–43); Luke 8:40–42, 49–56); raises the widow of Nain's son (Luke 7:11–17); raises Lazarus (John 11:1–45).

Chapter 20: Reading the Gospel According to Mark

1. Ernest Hemingway's, William Faulkner's
2. anarthrous
3. inclusio
4. terrified
5. repentance, baptism

6. torn apart, into, driven

7. immediately

Chapter 21: Reading the Luke-Acts Narrative

1. All apply.

2. open-ended question

3. true

4. distinct voices, narrator

5. ordinary people

6. tells, shows

7. forty, ten

8. Jesus, Holy Spirit

9. open-ended question

10. open-ended question

Chapter 22: Reading the Gospel According to John

1. Synoptic

2. prologue, epilogue, three

3. true

Chapter 23: Reading Romans

1. occasional, specific issues

2. orally, read privately

3. Spain

4. epistolary form

5. scholastic diatribe

6. questioner

7. midrash

8. thesis statement

9. individual, social

10. by faith

Chapter 24: Reading Paul's Early Epistles
Galatians

1. be under God's curse
2. apostolic authority
3. Jew, Gentile, slave, free, male, female

1 and 2 Thessalonians

4. three weeks, First Thessalonians
5. epideictic: the art of praise or blame
6. deliberative: the art of persuading an audience to take (or not take) an action

Chapter 25: Reading Paul's Corinthian Correspondence

1. five
2. Crispus, Gaius
3. Aquila, Priscilla
4. They had been exiled from Rome by the emperor Claudius.
5. next door to the home of Titus Justus
6. Sosthenes, Gallio
7. Nazirite, eighteen months
8. Factions and divisions are splitting the church. There is rampant sexual immorality.
9. false
10. third, comfort
11. patriarchal, monarchial, polytheistic, and slaveholding

Chapter 26: Reading Paul's Prison Epistles
Ephesians

1. golden, Asiatic, 202, parallel subordination
2. circular epistle or homily
3. performed

Philippians

4. Lydia, Zygaktis
5. baptizes, his family, city magistrate

Colossians

6. true
7. true
8. true

Philemon

9. Onesimus
10. rhetorical

Chapter 27: Reading Paul's Pastoral Letters
1 and 2 Timothy

1. personal correspondences
2. Ephesus, theology, ecclesiology
3. *paraenesis*
4. an authority figure
5. false doctrine or teaching
6. last will and testament
7. tender and compassionate

Titus

8. Galatians, 2 Corinthians, Titus
9. Crete
10. "Cretans are always liars, evil brutes, lazy gluttons"

Chapter 28: Reading the General Epistles and Letters
Hebrews

1. Don't have a clue

2. Jesus

3. homily, interprets, relevance, teaching

James

4. James, the "brother of the Lord"

5. commonsense advice

1 and 2 Peter

6. Pontus, Galatia, Cappadocia, Asia, Bithynia

7. Silas

8. teaching, persecution, truth

1, 2, and 3 John

9. excluded, not, the chosen lady and her children, beloved Gaius

Jude

10. false teachers

Chapter 29: Reading Revelation

1. the old order of things, Christ, good and evil, judgment, new heaven, new earth

2. threes, sevens

3. what was, what is, what will be

4. unveiling

5. Daniel

6. churches, angels or messengers

7. Pisidian Antioch, Colossae, Iconium

8. apocalyptic

9. on the island of Patmos in the Aegean Sea

10. garden of Eden, new Jerusalem